# WAR CARS
## British Armoured Cars in the First World War

*Frontispiece*     *'A Rolls in the desert was above rubies . . .' T.E. Lawrence*

*Front cover*     *A Rolls-Royce armoured car and a Daimler ambulance at a wayside dressing station near Guillemont in September 1916.*

# WAR CARS

## British Armoured Cars in the First World War

David Fletcher

*LONDON*   HER MAJESTY'S STATIONERY OFFICE

HMSO publications are available from:

**HMSO Publications Centre**
(Mail and telephone orders only)
PO Box 276, London, SW8 5DT
Telephone orders 01-622 3316
General enquiries 01-211 5656
(queuing system in operation for both numbers)

**HMSO Bookshops**
49 High Holborn, London, WC1V 6HB
01-211 5656 (Counter service only)
258 Broad Street, Birmingham, B1 2HE
021-643 3740
Southey House, 33 Wine Street, Bristol, BS1 2BQ
(0272) 264306
9–21 Princess Street, Manchester, M60 8AS
061-834 7201
80 Chichester Street, Belfast, BT1 4JY
(0232) 238451
71 Lothian Road, Edinburgh, EH3 9AZ
031-228 4181

**HMSO's Accredited Agents**
(see Yellow Pages)

*and through good booksellers*

# Contents

# Introduction

The mechanization of warfare – that is, the introduction of the armoured fighting vehicle – is associated in most people's minds with the invention of the tank, by the British, during the First World War. As a generalization this is perfectly reasonable although it fails to credit the efforts of a small band of men who had been fighting, and sometimes dying, in armoured vehicles for a good two years before the first tanks trundled into action. It also fails to acknowledge the work of other, earlier visionaries who had been preaching the gospel of mechanized warfare over the previous six decades.

That these pioneers should largely have been overlooked is not surprising. The men who built the first, primitive fighting machines worked in peacetime isolation in the face of a reactionary military establishment which dismissed them as crackpots. Even when the reality of war finally gave them their chance and armoured cars went into action they were too few in number to warrant much attention and, before long, scattered half-way across the globe, far from the main seat of war where the headlines were being made.

Towards the end of the First World War, when armoured cars returned to the Western Front, it was too late for them to claim their share of glory. The dramatic appearance of the tank had captured the public imagination to such an extent that those who kept faith with armour on wheels were virtually ignored, despite some staunch attempts to advertise their gallantry.

The situation is much the same today – the armoured car still has an important place in the family of combat vehicles but to the average citizen it is just another kind of tank. The modern armoured car is a very sophisticated machine with a key part to play in the concept of mobile warfare. It is highly mobile on and off the road, often amphibious and capable of carrying armaments every bit as destructive as a medium-sized battle tank. Indeed, the range of vehicles is so great and their abilities so diverse that the distinction between tanks and armoured cars is often blurred, even in the eyes of professional soldiers.

The original machines were quite the opposite, usually nothing more than lightly-armoured bodies fitted straight on to the chassis of civilian touring cars, but what chassis they were – Rolls-Royce, Lanchester, Clement-Talbot and Delaunay-Belleville were just a few classic thoroughbreds of their day. With ornate lamps and wire spoked wheels they brought an air of grace, style and opulence to the gruesome business of war.

Like the cars, the men who operated them were the cream of their generation; men like the Duke of Westmin-

ster (reputedly the wealthiest man in Britain) the MPs Wedgwood and Locker-Lampson, Wilding the lawn tennis star, Cherry-Garrard who had been with Scott in the Antarctic and, doyen of them all, motor buccaneer Charles Samson, the pioneer aviator. When the continental battle-front stagnated they 'searched the world for war' as Albert Stern wrote of them, and fought a war such as their brethren in the trenches could only dream of.

Yet for all their courage and glamour, these men and their armoured cars made little effective contribution to the outcome of the war. It could have been won without them but it would have been even more grim and perhaps less inspiring, less adventurous. Some homage is also due to the pioneer, whether renowned engineer or transparent rogue, who showed the way sixty years before the outbreak of the First World War. Furthermore it is essential to appreciate the part played by the Royal Navy in 1914 for, without the insistent enthusiasm of the sailors, Britain would have lagged far behind in the development of armoured cars and might never have invented the tank either. By the time the War Office unwillingly took over management of the cars an effective standard of design had been established and enviable reputations made in far flung outposts.

Besides the sleek and speedy armoured cars there were rugged armoured lorries, mounting larger guns, to support them in action and others designed to combat the aerial menace. At the other end of the scale was the motorcycle combination armed with a machine gun, which was very popular in the early part of the war despite the fact that it rarely proved serviceable in its intended role. All these are covered in this book along with various cars that originated in sister nations of the Empire and made contributions of their own.

The British were not the first to use armoured cars in the First World War and, compared with the French and Russians in particular, did not produce them in very large numbers, but they probably ranged further and wider than all the other combatant nations put together. Cars of a great variety of makes, many long since forgotten, with British crews fought in India, Russia, Ireland, France and from the Western Desert to the Persian Gulf.

Sadly no single example of a British armoured car of First World War vintage is known to survive anywhere today. There is an Autocar in Canada and a Vickers-Clyno motorcycle unit at the Imperial War Museum, but the flavour of the era may best be sampled at the Tank Museum at Bovington. Here, along with armoured vehicles of all ages, is a 1919 Peerless which exemplifies most of the features of those early cars, and a 1920 Rolls-Royce which differs little from its wartime predecessor. Both are preserved in full running order but, strictly speaking, they represent the immediate post-war period. Fortunately the Museum archives contain a wealth of documents and photographs that have been exploited in order to produce this book while the Fleet Air Arm Museum and Rolls-Royce Heritage have kindly allowed us to use material from their files. The author also wishes to acknowledge valuable help received over the years from many friends, notably Terry White, Just Probst and the late Colonel Bob Icks, and to offer special thanks to Charles Messenger for most generously compiling the appendix and David Parrott for his skilful interpretation of the various old drawings.

A work of this nature, which tries to cover a limited subject on a comprehensive scale, cannot hope to provide the reader with a detailed background on the war itself. It is a subject so vast, and open to such varieties of interpretation, that it can hardly be touched upon. Needless to say there is no shortage of published material that will enable the interested reader to delve deeper for himself.

# Prophets Without Honour

It was once fashionable for military historians to attempt to prove the pedigree of armoured fighting vehicles by tracing their lineage from the chariots and war-carts of the pre-Christian era. All this appears to prove is that men quickly learned to appreciate the need for protection and mobility on the battlefield. Since, to a large extent, mobility *is* protection, this factor could hardly be improved upon until something was developed that was both faster and more durable than the horse.

The horse was overtaken, in the first place, by the steam engine, initially as a stationary power plant and subsequently applied to ships, railways and road haulage, in that order. British industry led the way in the development of steam road traction from the middle years of the nineteenth century but its application to warfare took time to evolve and was never of much significance. Not that there was any shortage of ideas; one James Cowen, who is described as a philanthropist, came up with a design for an exceedingly uncharitable war machine, based upon a steam traction engine, at the time of the Crimean War; but it met with a very unenthusiastic response which roused Cowen to a most un-philanthropic outburst in the press:

---

## 'JAS. COWEN'S LAND & SEA LOCOMOTIVE STEAM RAM & BATTERY

Submitted to Lord Palmerston, the Premier of Great Britain and his colleagues, some of whom, as well as himself, highly approved of it in 1854, and by them referred to a Select Committee of the most experienced veterans of the age – supposed to be (?) but in reality washed-out Old Women and Senile Old Tabbies at Woolwich whither I caused the machine, models, plans &c. to be conveyed.

*MARK AT MY OWN EXPENSE!*

For Johnny Bull is a craving animal after his truly beloved God – money; and never parts with it willingly, but freely allows himself to be robbed of it by his rulers and taskmasters while he dozily dreams of freedom and liberty; and this idol of lucre he has only obtained by wading ankle deep in blood all over the world to get it – and this is his greatness.'

---

Cowen embellished his strange advertisment with the design of a cockerel above the exclamation 'Silence me – who can?' and a skull and crossbones with the cheerful legend 'The end of all is but to die, both rich and poor – both you and I'. Beneath this diatribe was a drawing, from

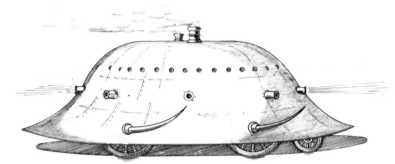

which the accompanying illustration is taken. One can see, underneath the helmet-shaped cover, a chassis sporting four even-sized wheels and the smaller pilot or steering-wheel often seen on early traction engines. Clouds of steam and smoke issue from a central chimney and from the muzzles of cannon facing fore and aft, while other guns are shown below a row of loopholes all around the hull. Even the spirit of Boadicea is summoned by enormous scythes which extend from the skirt of this strange machine. No wonder, as one report claims, Lord Palmerston described it as barbaric. If there ever was a scale model, and proper drawings, it is not surprising that the project was rejected. Even if the steam engine could be persuaded to operate over broken ground with all the extra weight, the muzzle-loading guns could hardly be served on the move and there appears to be no allowance for recoil at all. The gunners, sandwiched between the outer shell and the boiler, would probably have been roasted alive.

For the next thirty years there was very little progress in military mechanization of any sort, apart from a steady trickle of traction engines purchased for evaluation. These were only intended for haulage work and nothing was done to mobilize the fighting arms. However, the latter part of the nineteenth century was very much the age of the bicycle in both public and military circles. A number of volunteer regiments formed cyclist battalions which could be seen, on annual exercises, pedalling around the countryside or stepping into action with a folded bicycle strapped to the back of each trooper. A cycling enthusiast from Leicester, G.H. Waite, who worked for the Humber Company in Nottingham, produced a four wheeled quadricycle with saddles and pedals for three, which mounted an air-cooled

1  *Waite's Maxim quadricycle of 1888.*

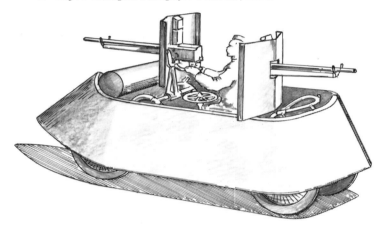

2  *E.J. Pennington's design for a war car, 1896.*

3  *Frederick Simms demonstrating his Motor Scout, Richmond, 1899.*

Maxim machine gun in addition to rifles for the crew. The date was 1888 but, despite the fact that military cycling was popular all over Europe and the United States, his idea never caught on.

It was the dramatic appearance of the internal combustion engine, as applied to self-moving machines, that first motivated inventors to consider proper combat vehicles. It is, perhaps, a little unfortunate that the first person to do so in England was not only an American but a first class con-man to boot. Edward Joel Pennington (as he chose to call himself) was a minister's son from Indiana, born in 1858. After six years apprenticeship to a pattern maker he discovered that floating spurious business projects and selling worthless patents was a far more agreeable, and livelier, way of making a fortune and went at it with a vengeance. Although his stock-in-trade was wooden-pulley making machinery he was not afraid to branch out into freight elevators, automobiles and even airships, from which last venture he acquired his nickname. His stature, manners and flamboyant dress, together with an eye for publicity and a persuasive tongue, did not necessarily bespeak integrity but he had a natural talent for exploiting greed in others and all the conscience of a starving wolf. He made a fortune or two in the process but was obliged to keep moving with half of small-town America hard on his heels. Yet, long before any sane person would have done so, Pennington seems to have recognized the potential of the private motorcar market and soon concentrated his efforts on this to the exclusion of his other projects.

In 1895 he came to Britain. Whether it was getting too hot for him in the United States, or he was attracted by the activities of H.J. Lawson, it is impossible to say, but the latter seems as likely a reason as any. 1895 was the year of motoring emancipation in Britain, with the repeal of the 'Red Flag Act', and Harry Lawson had set himself to benefit from it. He was a British impresario who planned to corner the market in motorcar production by the simple expedient of buying up the patent rights to every kind of motor vehicle that he could lay his hands on. These rights could then be leased to other British manufacturers who, in theory, might go on paying indefinitely for the privilege. Whatever Lawson's qualities as a businessman may have been he was no match for 'Airship' Pennington who took him for £100,000 and then proceeded, by bluff and sharp practice, to carve quite a name for himself in the British motor industry. Some Pennington cars were produced but they looked as outlandish as they were unreliable, while the few that were sold went a long way to establishing a reputation as the 'world's worst car'. Even so, in 1896, the American produced a perspective drawing showing an armoured car capable of mounting two machine guns behind shields, on a chassis that was completely encased in a protective skirt of armour. One feature that Pennington pioneered to some effect was the large-section pneumatic tyre, which did not appear again on the commercial market for about forty years; these were essential on a Pennington because it had no springs, but they failed to live up to the inventor's claim that they were unpuncturable! Many harsh things have been said about Pennington, all of them well deserved, but he should be given some credit for these tyres and for the foresight that led him to suggest an armoured motorcar at this time.

Another motoring pioneer who got caught up in Lawson's great enterprise was a Briton, Frederick R. Simms, but unlike Pennington he was a gifted and reputable engineer. His high tension magneto was considered a major contribution to motorcar design and he held the British rights to the valuable Daimler patents which, in due course, he sold to Lawson. Like most Victorian engineers, Simms cast his net wide and dabbled in everything from tramcars to farm machinery, but he claims our attention as the first man in the world to actually produce a motorized fighting vehicle, albeit of dubious combat potential. Simms' invention, the Motor Scout, was really little more than a motorized version of Waite's military quadricycle. Simms, smartly dressed in suit and bowler, demonstrated it at the Richmond Automobile Show in 1899. The machine on which it was based was a typical motor quadricycle of the period on which the rider sat on a normal cycle-saddle above the frame with conventional handlebar controls. The passenger usually occupied a more comfortable seat between the front forks, set low enough for the driver to see over his passenger's head. It was manufactured by the Beeston Motor Cycle Company of Coventry and powered by a De Dion type 1½ hp engine mounted at the rear. On Simms' version the front seat was removed and in its place was a tripod mounting for an air-cooled Maxim machine gun with an ammunition tray beneath it. There was no protection for the rider beyond a small detachable shield fitted to the gun. The military authorities took no notice whatsoever and nothing more was heard of the Motor Scout, although Simms did not lose interest. By the end of the year Britain was plunged into the Boer War.

The forty or so years that separated the South African War from the Crimean War had been years of great social and industrial progress. The steamship, the telegraph, the railway, and very nearly, the traction engine, had made a slight impression on the earlier conflict but by 1899 they had all grown up and been joined by the machine gun, wireless and breech-loading weapons of all calibres. Armoured trains, although hardly a new idea, were accepted at once but attitudes within the British Army had failed to keep pace with technical progress. A few traction engines were sent out to the Cape to support the animal-drawn supply columns but they were greeted with a distinct lack of enthusiasm at the front. The majority were operated by No.45 (Steam Road Transport) Company, Royal Engineers, under Captain G.P. Schofield, RE but they found little work to do. Official distrust, user inexperience and general ridicule kept them in the background for months, yet in the first flush of enthusiasm a curious step had been taken. Most of the engines supplied to the Sappers came

from the Leeds works of John Fowler and Co., one of Britain's leading builders of steam road engines, and shortly after the outbreak of war the firm had accepted a revolutionary contract for six armoured road trains, based on their successful B5 class road locomotive. Known also as the Lion type these engines weighed about 17 tons in their unarmoured form and ran on seven-foot diameter hind wheels. Rated, in the curious terminology of the day, at 10 nominal horsepower, they were quite capable of shifting close on one hundred tons at a time. The logic that led to the appearance of the armoured version no doubt owed a lot to the theories that first produced the armoured railway train – that is, a means of securing communication in territory that was vulnerable to hostile raiders.

Each engine was protected all over with steel plates up to a quarter of an inch thick, produced by Cammells of Sheffield; this plate was capable of stopping a Mauser bullet at close range. The engines were designed to run on coal, wood or oil fuel and had three optional gear ratios that offered speeds between two and six miles per hour. A complete train would consist of an engine with three or four armoured wagons of ingenious design. Each wagon was fitted with hinged side plates, but open at the top. There

4    *A Fowler armoured road locomotive built for service in South Africa.*

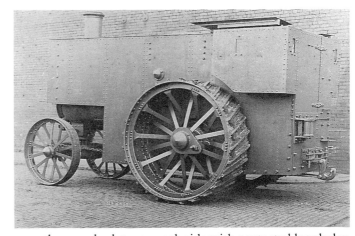

were three such plates on each side with protected loopholes for riflemen to shoot through, so that the train could be used as a sort of armoured personnel carrier to bring forward troops under fire, to secure a bridge or river crossing, carry out flanking operations or cover a withdrawal. If stores were carried instead, the plates were lowered inwards to form an overall roof while rear doors and portable ramps were provided so that a small howitzer could be winched aboard by the engine if required. Most of the design work was undertaken by a young Captain of Royal Engineers called Nugent who went on to make a name for himself in the field of military transportation. The odd thing, in the light of its reactionary reputation, was that the War Office should sanction such an idea so early in the war, when ordinary traction engines had yet to prove themselves.

The first complete train was demonstrated to the press at Leeds in May 1900 and two had arrived in South Africa by January 1901, another pair following at the end of the year. By this time traction engines had become an established part of the transport scene. Their efficiency became a byword, particularly when it was appreciated that they were not subject to the various diseases that could decimate animal teams on the veldt. It was also discovered that even unarmoured locomotives were rarely attacked by the Boer raiders, who found them very difficult to destroy. For this reason, among others, it seems that the armoured types were never used as intended and the plating was removed from the four locomotives, which finished the war as conventional engines. The two remaining trains stayed in Britain, where the armoured wagons were used for some years after the war to test loads during subsequent military traction engine trials. In passing it is worth noting that Fowlers supplied another pair of traction engines with armoured cabs to the Uganda Railways for use on construction projects where thick undergrowth, wild animals and unruly tribesmen posed a threat to the well-being of drivers.

The Boer War was too good a chance for Edward Pennington to miss. Early in 1900 he was in New York but later in the year he returned to Britain where he could be found, early each morning, testing his latest creation in Richmond Park. This was a robust machine that looked like a heavy-duty version of Simms' quadricycle. It was of tubular frame construction with the leading wheels held in cycle-type forks. Saddles were provided for a crew of five or six, and a set of pedals at the rear were for starting the engine. Pennington engines were built in defiance of all the principles established by Benz, Daimler and other pioneers (to avoid patent claims). The two cylinders were formed from 5-inch-diameter steel pipes, about 12 inches long. The ignition system employed what Pennington called the 'long mingling spark' which, in effect, generated a spark within generous margins either side of top dead centre. Thus it was bound to fire at some point during the stroke and did away with the need for a magneto. Pennington also chose to avoid the complications of radiator and water pump by jacketing each cylinder in a water-filled sleeve, fed from a header tank at the front, which worked well until the coolant boiled away. This tank also formed a sort of shield, the only protection available to the crew, although Pennington claimed that the finished product would be covered at front and sides by an armoured skirt. Never one to undersell himself the bold American claimed a top speed of 60 mph and explained to the press that his car could mount two Maxim or Colt machine guns and carry up to eight men. He went on to say that five more cars were ready as soon as the government wanted them.

The technical journals of the day appeared to be impressed although *The Autocar* which usually supported Pennington doubted if the ground clearance was sufficient. Since he was adept at handling reporters and a master of public relations it is unwise to believe any of his claims.

5    One of the armoured road trains during trials in the Leeds area in May 1900. In addition to the three armoured wagons the engine is hauling two 6-inch howitzers.

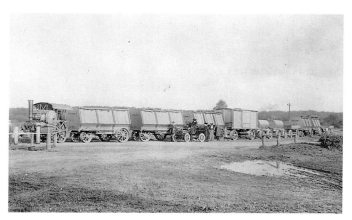

6    No less than five armoured wagons form part of the test train for this Fowler D2 class traction engine during trials in 1903.

7    Pennington, on the right, with his 'armoured' car in Richmond Park.

Certainly those he aired on another design, which was illustrated in the *Chicago Tribune* in July 1900, were as outrageous as ever. Yet the car which he showed in London certainly did exist, at least as a chassis and, once again, it is the wheels that most impress a modern observer; the wire-spoked rims, of 22-inch diameter, carried 5-inch section balloon tyres which, as usual, served in lieu of suspension. In 1901 Pennington was reported to be testing another armoured car in the north of England but nothing is known of its design. For the last ten years of his life this colourful charlatan returned home to continue his dubious career against a background of bankruptcy and jail as his past steadily caught up with him.

F.R. Simms hit the headlines again in 1901 with a neat little machine which was essentially an armoured car on rails. Powered by a 7 hp water-cooled engine, driving through a three-speed Panhard gearbox that gave a top speed of 30 mph in each direction, it was designed as a scouting vehicle to keep railway lines clear of raiders or sabotage. It looked more like a large galvanized bathtub on wheels than anything else and was capable of mounting a one-pounder Pom-Pom, a Maxim gun and a searchlight, with a crew of four. Tested on a section of line along the north shore of the river Medway, it was said to have been exported to Nairobi although details of its fate are unknown.

John Fowler and Co. built four more armoured traction engines for the India Office in 1902, presumably for convoy work on the North West Frontier. Based on the B8 class compound road locomotive, the armour protection was limited to the footplate and the working parts above the boiler. One engine was fitted with a five-ton crane on the front axle and they all came supplied with trains of steel-bodied open wagons. Unfortunately no details of their service careers have yet been found.

8   *Fred Simms takes aim with a Maxim gun during a demonstration of his armoured rail car.*

9   *One of the Fowler armoured engines built for India – the one fitted with a jib – towing four of the special wagons in a pre-delivery trial.*

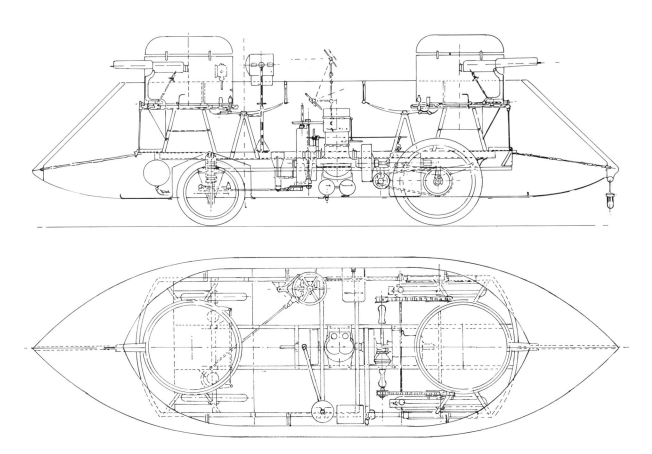

*10 A copy of the drawing of Simms' War Car which appeared in* The Autocar *in April 1902.*

The first true, petrol-driven armoured car appeared in Britain in 1902, designed by the redoubtable Fred Simms and built by Vickers, Sons and Maxim. Inspired by the Boer War, it was completed too late to see active service even if it had been adopted by the military. Its appearance seems to owe something to the original Pennington design although, fortunately, this did not extend to the mechanical arrangements. These were both original and, given the early date, quite successful. Known as the Simms Motor War Car it was designed expressly as a fighting machine from the wheels upwards. It was a large, heavy vehicle; 28 ft long, 8 ft wide and 10 ft high with a chassis that could accept a payload of 12 tons. Power was provided by a Simms-Daimler four-cylinder engine rated at 16 hp which drove through a Canstatt four-speed gearbox, giving a top speed of 9 mph. The driver was stationed amidships and, under fire, he was supposed to keep his head down and observe by means of mirrors, which would have been very tricky. A drawing released by Simms and published in '*The Autocar*', showed the machine with a Maxim gun turret at each end but, when it was shown off to the press outside the Crystal Palace in April 1902 no turrets were fitted. Instead it mounted a Vickers-Maxim one-pounder Pom-Pom at the rear, with two water-cooled Maxim machine guns at the front. A small, air-cooled Maxim was also clipped to the side of the hull alongside the driver (and loaded with blanks) which the inventor loosed off every now and then

*11 Outside the Crystal Palace Simms' War Car contains an elegant crew but there is not a uniform in sight.*

when interest appeared to be flagging. The armoured hull was made in the form of an elliptical skirt, tapered at each end to form a ram and attached to the frame by means of four inverted leaf springs supported on trestles. This was intended to reduce vibration but Simms discovered that it also caused the entire body to sway alarmingly fore and aft when it was under way, so he added stays at either end.

In addition to the armament the car was designed to carry twelve infantrymen, but the only means of getting aboard was a rope ladder slung over the side. Meanwhile, with the Boer war over, a new threat was looming. Certain elements in French society were openly discussing the prospect of invading Britain with a fleet of submarines. The War Car was therefore advertised as a means of mobile coast defence, which led the press in some countries to print fanciful drawings of it, many times larger than life, taking on everything from airships to warships with guns poking out from every imaginable orifice. Despite this public interest the War Office did not respond at all, indeed it even failed to send a representative to the demonstration, so that Simms abandoned his interest in the further development of military vehicles.

The first years of the new century witnessed a technological struggle between steam and internal combustion engines for road transport, both civil and military – a struggle that the petrol engine steadily won. The army concentrated on testing a variety of samples rather than building up a big fleet, but motor lorries were becoming a common sight on Britain's highways. The same could not be said of the private motorcar, which was still regarded as a rich man's toy of very little practical value. It was left to enterprising individuals within the services to experiment with their own machines and some private cars turned up at annual camps with a machine gun in tow. Sir Percy Scott, the famous naval gunnery expert, even went so far as to fit his Wolseley with a Maxim gun in the front, and an enormous, bearded matelot to handle it.

In 1903 there appeared a curious armoured version of the three-wheeled Ivel tractor. The Ivel was the brainchild of Dan Albone of Biggleswade and it was Britain's first successful farm tractor. Fitted with a horizontal two-cylinder engine and a gearbox that gave one speed in either direction, the basic layout was not very different from a modern tractor. The version Albone offered to the War Office was armoured all over, with a raised cab at the rear to cover the driver. The back of the cab was composed of nine folding steel plates which could be swung down and outwards to form a broad shield. The idea seems to have been as much humane as aggressive since the tractor could be driven on to the battlefield and halted under fire to provide cover behind which stretcher bearers might safely rescue casualties. Apparently the Royal Marines showed some interest and it was demonstrated to potential customers from abroad, but Albone died in 1906 and the firm stuck to more conventional merchandise thereafter.

By 1906 armoured cars were starting to appear in Europe.

12  *A privately owned Panhard towing a Maxim gun at a summer camp.*

13  *The 10 hp Wolseley of Admiral Sir Percy Scott mounting a Maxim machine gun.*

14  *The armoured Ivel tractor marked with the Red Cross and with the rear shield partly open.*

15 *The Armstrong-Whitworth armoured car outside the Elswick works. Notice the similarity between its front wheels and those of the gun.*

16 *The Driggs-Schroeder automatic cannon mounted on the special Maudslay demonstration vehicle.*

Few were actually adopted by the armed forces but some were ingenious designs that set the pattern of armoured cars for many years. The next British armoured car was built by the Newcastle armaments firm of Sir W.G. Armstrong, Whitworth & Co. in the same year. The designer was a young ex-naval engineer officer, Walter Gordon Wilson, whose remarkable Wilson-Pilcher cars were already being produced by the Tyneside firm. Wilson's military car, which seems to have been partially armoured, was demonstrated as a gun tractor although it was claimed that a Pom-Pom could be fitted if required. Wilson was a transmission expert, a pioneer of the epicyclic gear system for motorcars, and his armoured machine as a consequence featured a four-speed epicyclic box driving to the rear axle from a four-cylinder engine at the front. Apart from the fact that there was no effective protection for the upper half of the driver when he was sitting at the wheel, the car did have some interesting features. One was a small recovery winch and earth anchor on the left side, while the wheels were identical to those normally fitted to field guns. The idea was that a car damaging a wheel in action could save itself by taking a spare from the nearest field gun. What the Royal Artillery, with their tradition of saving the guns at all costs, thought of this is not recorded. In the event it did not matter very much since the car failed to generate any interest, although its designer went on to become one of the co-inventors of the tank and an acknowledged expert in the field of tank transmissions for the next thirty years.

The Maudslay Motor Company of Coventry supplied a specially modified car chassis in 1909. It was fitted, as a demonstration vehicle, with an American-made Driggs-Schroeder automatic cannon, but it could not be considerd as a serious attempt to build a fighting machine.

Now, with war clouds gathering, things went strangely quiet. Interest in motor vehicles continued to grow and a subsidy scheme for army lorries was introduced in 1911, but there was still no official recognition of a need for armoured fighting vehicles. Even the sporadic and unco-ordinated attempts to build them privately ceased for a while. Indeed, the next two types to appear in the British Isles were improvised civilian concoctions built in response to particular emergencies.

In the summer of 1911 there was a serious transport strike in Liverpool which soon got out of hand. The police reported riot and riotous damage on a large scale while two men were shot during an attack on a prison van. The Army was called in to assist but in the meantime the Merseyside force took a radical step of its own. A commercial Hallford lorry was obtained and fitted with a large protected body of timber planks and wire netting which could carry a squad of policemen in relative security from the bottles and brickbats that the 'hooligan men and women', as the police described them, hurled at the vehicle. A press report described how officers could jump out swiftly to arrest offenders who were bundled, doubtless with little ceremony, into the back of the truck.

The Liberal Home Rule Bill of 1912 caused similar unrest in Ireland, but here the threat was posed by the Loyalist element, supported to some extent by the Army. The problem rumbled on for the next two years and a Loyalist militia was formed to concentrate the opposition. Much given to parading with rifles, they also fielded, at least on one occasion, a Model T Ford car with a Colt machine gun mounted at the back. It was posed for the press, surrounded by gunmen, to drive the point home but with the outbreak of war in 1914 the whole matter was shelved, only to break out again on the Republican side in 1916.

Britain seemed to have turned its back on armoured cars and in Western Europe they only toyed with a few prototypes, but the Czarist army in Russia showed considerable interest. Lacking a worthwhile motor industry of its own Russia was obliged to buy from abroad and had been doing so since 1904. The first armoured car supplied to the

*17   Escorted by troops and followed by a convoy of tramcars the Liverpool police sally forth in their protected Hallford lorry.*

*18   Supported by 'infantry' with ancient single-shot Remingtons the Loyalists pose their Colt carrying Ford T in Ireland.*

Imperial government came from France but they managed to produce one of their own, a Russo-Baltique, in 1912. In the following year they ordered their first British armoured car from Armstrong Whitworths. The hull was of riveted construction and stately appearance, surmounted by a small, drum-shaped turret mounting a water cooled machine gun. Fitted with wooden spoked wheels and solid tyres its performance must have been poor, especially on the dreadful Russian roads, yet one authoritative source claims that thirty-six of them were delivered over the next three years. The suggestion that there was more than one is supported by a photograph, taken in Vladivostok in 1919, which shows a car of very similar design, with some typical Russian modifications to the hull, bogged down to the axles in a muddy city street.

In early 1914 the War Office Mechanical Transport Committee, which had been functioning since 1902, submitted a draft report for the attention of the General Staff that, among other things, offered to undertake a comparative study of contemporary armoured cars, in view of developments on the Continent. They got a dusty reply; 'there are many other things of far greater importance and, therefore, this matter might be allowed to stand over for the present'. The report was never published; the outbreak of war in August 1914 really was a thing of far greater importance.

20 *Carrying the winged-wheel symbol of Russian armoured car units this heavily modified Armstrong-Whitworth was well and truly stuck when it was photographed in Vladivostock in 1919.*

19 *Posing again; one of the Armstrong-Whitworth armoured cars supplied to Russia in 1913.*

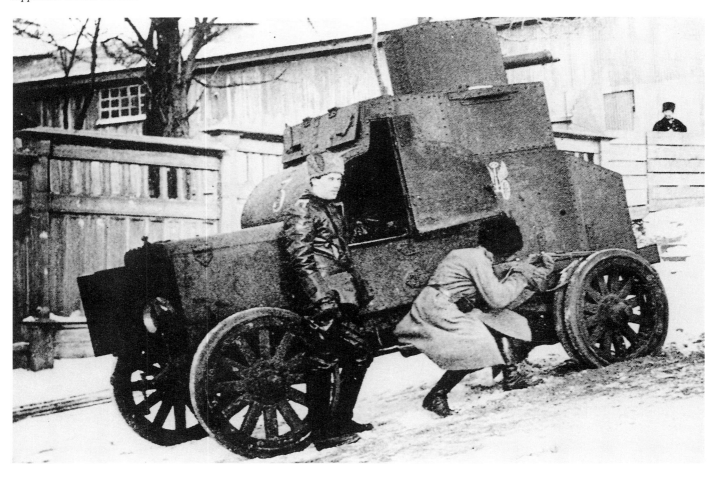

# CHAPTER 2
# Navy Days

The Eastchurch Squadron of the Royal Naval Air Service was based at the airfield of that name on the Isle of Sheppey. It was commanded by a slight, bewhiskered firebrand called Charles Rumney Samson who, in January 1912, made the first ever take-off from a ship when he launched his Short Seaplane down a ramp fitted to a turret of the cruiser HMS Africa. Samson was a fighter in the mould of Drake and Nelson and he chafed at the role allotted to his squadron when the war broke out. By official decree it had been decided that the air arm of the War Office, the Royal Flying Corps, should accompany the British Expeditionary Force to France while the Royal Naval Air Service remained in Britain to defend the homeland from the Zeppelin threat.

Samson argued that the best way to deal with the airships was to attack them at their home bases so, with the connivance of the First Lord of the Admiralty, Winston Churchill, he took his squadron across to Dunkirk where they could operate within range of the Zeppelin sheds at Dusseldorf and Cologne. Naturally the squadron had a complement of motor transport consisting of ten lorries and a similar number of touring cars which belonged to some of the officers, and all this equipment went to France too. Two of Samson's three brothers served with the squadron and the Mercedes of Felix Samson was soon fitted with a spare Maxim gun for use against aerial and terrestrial targets.

During the months of fluid warfare that preceded the establishment of the trench lines, the situation in north east France and Belgium was wide open. The northern flank of the invading German army was screened by cavalry, motor and cyclist patrols which the intrepid airmen encountered on their motorized excursions. These trips were undertaken as an adjunct to the flying operations, to reconnoitre new landing sites and rescue pilots brought down in disputed territory. Following an encounter with a carload of Germans Felix Samson designed a form of armour protection for his car, which now became known as the Iron Duke. The plate was supplied and fitted by a shipbuilding firm, Forges et Chantiers de France at Dunkirk. In reality the protection offered was more moral than physical since true armour plate was not available and they were forced to use ordinary boilerplate which was only effective against rifle bullets at ranges above 500 yards. In the meantime Commander Samson had obtained two machine guns and four gunners from the French Army and these were used to equip two more unarmoured cars so that more effective patrols could be mounted. Before long a Rolls-Royce was fitted with armour to the same design as the Mercedes but Samson appreciated that a better type of armoured car could be designed, given time and the proper facilities. He forwarded his ideas to the Admiralty along with a request for some real armour plate and also asked for reinforcements in the form of a detachment of Royal Marines.

The transport fleet that supported the Eastchurch Squadron consisted for the most part of lorries that had been converted from London General Omnibus Company double-deck B Type buses and the Samson brothers now took two of these in hand for conversion into armoured transports for the Marines. Once again the work was carried out by the Dunkirk shipyard and the result was a very effective-looking vehicle with protection for the radiator and cab, while the rest of the body was encased in sloping steel plates which could protect up to a dozen riflemen as

21  *This cartoon by S.C.H. Davis shows the image that Samson's men had of themselves during training.*

22  *Men of the RNAS sorting stores alongside one of the Samson brothers' Maxim equipped tourers in Flanders.*

long as they knelt down. In practice the modified buses proved too slow to keep up with the cars so they usually served as mobile strongpoints to guard the crossroads outside Samson's headquarters at Hazebrouck. Late in September 1914 the Squadron was joined by a new officer, Lord Annesley, who brought his own home-made armoured car with him. Samson spoke well of the design but not the workmanship, since bits of armour used to drop off as it went along the road so, in due course, it was stripped down and used for despatch work.

The controller of the Admiralty Air Department in London was Commodore Murray Sueter, a pioneer of both airship and submarine construction. Samson describes him as a real live member of society who did not suffer from hidebound ideas. It was up to Sueter to implement the request for better armoured cars and he began by putting forward a suggestion that fifty should be made, in a paper dated 11 September 1914. Commenting in the margin his superior, Winston Churchill, raised the number to one hundred but the final proposal called for sixty armoured cars with forty support cars of the following varieties:

**60 Fighting Cars** armed with 1 Maxim, mountings for 2 if required, men with rifles and protected with 4 mm armour plating.
These are proposed of the following makes:
18 Rolls-Royce 40/50 hp.
21 Clement-Talbot 25/50 hp.
21 Wolseley 30 hp.

**40 Non-fighting Cars**
4 ambulances, Wolseley Army type to maintain connection between advanced and permanent bases for wounded.
8 cars for aeroplane and motor car spare parts, breakdown tools etc.
8 general service cars.
20 waggons for provisions, fuel, stores etc. for advanced bases.

The unresolved question concerned the design. There was no worthwhile fund of experience to begin with, beyond what Samson had accumulated, but Sueter chose to ignore

*23   Commander Samson's first armoured Rolls-Royce in the Dunkirk shipyard where it was built.*

*25   A copy of the original sketch, submitted to Churchill, for an Admiralty designed armoured car.*

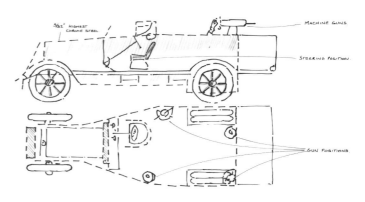

*24   Riflemen of the Royal Marines in one of the armoured B type buses.*

*26   A Rolls-Royce chassis fitted with a mock-up wooden body to show the layout of the new armoured cars.*

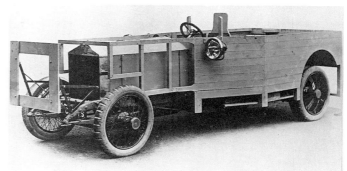

this in favour of a design put forward by Lord Wimborne and the Admiralty Air Department. A crude sketch was translated into a full size wooden mock-up on a Rolls-Royce chassis and the production cars were similar, with minor variations to suit the different makes of chassis. Sheets of armour plate covered the sides and top of the engine, continuing around the sides and rear of the body at dashboard height, 4 mm nickel chrome steel was used throughout although the only member of the crew to be offered complete protection was the driver who sat beneath a box shaped hood. The remainder were dangerously exposed unless they chose to lie on the floor and even then they were vulnerable to fire directed at them from the upper storeys and roofs of buildings. Sixty Maxim machine guns were collected from the fleet and each car had two fixed mounting points, at the offside and the rear, from which they could be fired.

*27 An armoured Talbot built at Sheerness. This one has a framework fitted over the body either to cut wire or support a canvas cover.*

The Wolseley cars had a sloping plate over the radiator while the Rolls-Royces and some Talbots had hinged doors and some effort was also made to protect the tyres. The chassis of all three makes had been tested with weights equivalent to that of the armoured hull and a payload of 30 cwt but the only modification considered necessary was the fitting of Dunlop, or Warland, dual rims on the rear axles. The armour was fitted at the Royal Naval Dockyard at Sheerness and as soon as the cars were ready they were shipped to France. The first group was commanded by the aptly named Royal Marine Major Risk, the second by Lieutenant Commander Josiah Wedgwood MP, RNVR. While these units worked up Samson continued to fight with the original cars, supplemented by some French armoured cars of similar design. Co-operating with French troops around Douai they had a number of scraps with German cavalry but operations were often hampered where trenches had been dug across the roads. The cars were too heavy to work their way round across country and these hold-ups were a portent of things to come.

Early in October the Germans were threatening Antwerp so an operation was mounted to evacuate the Royal Marine defenders in a convoy of ex-London buses that arrived at Dunkirk complete with their original crews, who had volunteered for active service. Samson was ordered to get the convoy through and he set out with a force of eleven armoured cars and the two armoured buses. The 90-mile route via Bruges was vulnerable to enemy raids for most of the way so the commander sent some of the cars on ahead to station themselves along the road and join up with the main column as it passed by. The remaining cars were scattered

*28 A Rolls-Royce armoured car of the RNAS surrounded by an admiring group of army officers.*

among the buses with a strong head and rearguard, while Marine riflemen travelled in every sixth bus, there being seventy buses in all. Samson was so impressed by the skill of the busmen that, when they broke the journey at Bruges for the night, he had all the buses driven into the barrack square for safety. The officer commanding the bus column despaired of ever getting them out again, for there was no room to spare but, left to their own devices, the crews had their fleet out and lined up on the road within twenty minutes of the order to go on the following morning. Just outside Antwerp the convoy was halted and Samson reorganized the column for a grand entry. Leading the way came the eleven armoured cars, followed by the two armoured buses and the seventy London doubledeckers, each still in the blue and white liveries of the Gearless and Metropolitan Electric Tramway Companies, subsidiaries of the LGOC.

The aircraft of the Eastchurch Squadron also went to Antwerp, where they were stationed on the racecourse with the armoured cars. Although the enemy was pressing hard the cars found little to do. They spent most of the time lying up at places behind the lines to act as strong points for the Marines to fall back on, or to lead local counterattacks should the need arise. It was clear that this defensive role did not suit them at all so they returned to France shortly afterwards where opportunities for action still remained.

By the middle of October the Dunkirk shipyard had delivered another new vehicle to the unit, the latest of Samson's designs. It was simply one of the erstwhile B Type buses, masquerading as a lorry, which now carried a Vickers semi-automatic three-pounder gun in the rear. The sides of the body could be folded flat to increase the floor space when in action but no armour was fitted at all. Since

30    *Crowds gather in an Antwerp square to admire a line up of RNAS Wolseleys. Both armoured cars and tenders are seen here.*

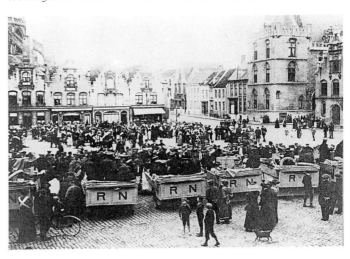

31    *The original 3-pdr gun lorry, based on a B type bus chassis and photographed at Dunkirk.*

29    *Two armoured Wolseleys lead the bus column into Antwerp.*

his transport fleet was now somewhat depleted by these conversions, and replacements were not forthcoming, Samson resorted to piracy. An Army Service Corps convoy was discovered, unguarded, in Poperinghe while the drivers took their lunch and the Navy men moved in. Two lorries were appropriated by the simple expedient of painting the letters RNAS on the sides and driving them away. They might have got more had not the soldiers returned!

The three-pounder lorry went into action for the first time on 17 October in support of the Life Guards near Westroosebeke. Samson was clearly delighted with it since a few rounds were quite sufficient to drive the Germans from a farmhouse which they were trying to fortify. Indeed, as work for the armoured cars became harder and harder to find the lorry proved ever more useful, so it was joined by a similar type on a Mercedes-Daimler chassis which also featured a shield for the gun and limited protection for the driver. At the same time six of the Admiralty cars, mostly Talbots, were modified at Dunkirk to Samson's design. The work involved fitting extra panels all round the top of the

fighting compartment, sloped inwards to give much better protection for the crew. Hinged vision flaps were provided for the driver and a pair of Maxim guns could be carried, pointing fore and aft. The cars were camouflage-painted and given names that recalled some of the squadron's earlier actions, but they were completed too late to be of much use. A Rolls-Royce was altered in much the same way and served as a towing vehicle for another three-pounder gun, which was mounted on a small two-wheeled carriage.

Samson's final design was in many ways his most impressive although it never saw action. Based on the chassis of a 5-ton Mercedes lorry it featured a totally enclosed armoured body armed with six Maxim machine guns. Behind the cab a raised lookout tower was provided for the commander, while a rear facing steering position enabled it to be driven backwards from a tight spot without the need to turn around. Describing it in his war memoir, *Fights and Flights*, Samson claims that it had many attributes of the tank, except for the ability to travel away from the roads.

As 1914 drew to a close it was clear that the nature of the war was changing, the scattered slit trenches were linking up and closing in on both sides, and soon there would be no room for freebooters of Samson's stamp. In any case the armoured cars were a side issue compared with the important work his squadron was doing in the air. In due course they had to give up the cars and take their aircraft out to the Mediterranean where they saw action at Gallipoli. Fortunately this was not the end of the armoured cars. Samson had presented his case very well and, back in Britain, new men were preparing to take up his torch and carry it to the far corners of the Empire.

The cars produced by Samson and the Admiralty bore all the hallmarks of a panic measure. In terms of design if not performance, better cars had appeared ten years earlier. The limitations of the improvised cars were readily appreciated; the vulnerability of the crew and the awkwardness of

*32  Samson's Mercedes-Daimler also mounted a 3-pdr gun but the cab was lightly armoured.*

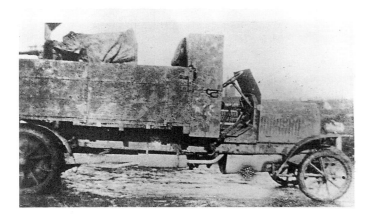

*33  HMS Aniche, one of the Admiralty Talbots modified by Samson at Dunkirk.*

*34  The massive armoured Mercedes lorry designed by Samson and his team being swung aboard ship.*

35   *One of the three turreted Delaunay-Bellevilles photographed at the Forges et Chantier works.*

the machine gun mountings made them death traps on wheels. Clearly the answer was a totally enclosed hull with a turret for the weapon. Seuter mentions a Captain Nickerson, based at Dunkirk, who first put the idea of a turreted car to the Admiralty but, he claims, the difficulty of bending thin armour plate had not been solved at this stage. While the renowned steelmakers, Beardmores, addressed this problem, Forges et Chantiers at Dunkirk got to work on some prototypes which may have been the result of Nickerson's proposal. Three Delaunay-Belleville chassis were delivered to the shipyard by the firm's English agent, probably direct from the factory at St Denis. Delaunay-Belleville was to the French what Rolls-Royce still is to the British – quite simply the best car in the world – with a powerful six-cylinder engine behind a stylish round radiator. They were fitted with turreted bodies, probably of boilerplate. The turrets were drum-shaped and mounted a single, water-cooled Maxim, while the front of the cab was well sloped to increase the effective protection. There is no record of them ever entering service in France but they certainly came back to Britain where, in due course, one of them served a most useful purpose that its designer could never have foreseen. Meanwhile Beardmores announced to the Admiralty that the knack of bending light armour plate without cracking it had been acquired and production of a new generation of armoured cars could begin.

36   *The prototype of the famous turreted Admiralty pattern Rolls-Royce armoured car.*

The Admiralty design for a turreted armoured car was one of the most successful and influential ever produced; it was copied, in principle, all over the world. Coupled with the eminently reliable Rolls-Royce Silver Ghost chassis it became one of the most effective wheeled fighting vehicles of the age. The armoured hull clung to the outline of the original car while the shallow, bevel-topped, turret set it off to perfection. A Maxim, and later a Vickers machine gun, mounted on an internal fork, protruded through an aperture in the front of the turret with a complementary hinged flap in the rear. There was a hatch in the top of the turret and access to the hull was through a pair of doors in the rear, each split horizontally like stable doors. The driver had a hinged visor plate with slits in it which enabled him to drive under fire, while moveable armoured shutters protected his side lookouts and the various pistol ports around the hull. In addition to the normal controls each car was fitted with a novel internal starting device, working off the flywheel, and a lever which operated armoured doors covering the radiator. Naturally these could not be kept closed for too long due to the risk of overheating, but the very speed of the cars – upwards of 50 mph even with full armour – meant that they were never under continuous fire for very long. In order to keep its weight to a minimum the rear end of the car was not enclosed. Instead it formed an open tray with a hinged tailgate and stowage lockers, all of

wood. The petrol tank was mounted beneath the floor of this tray but, in common with most cars of the period, it fed a header tank behind the dashboard by means of a pressure pump.

With a nominal crew of three and an all-up weight of around four tons the cars had a respectable performance and a remarkable ability to operate over all kinds of terrain. Early experience indicated that the springs were under considerable strain so these were strengthened, while cars destined to serve in France were fitted with tyres filled with Rubberine, a self-sealing compound that was supposed to prevent punctures. With a view to crossing trenches each car carried two detachable planks, in the form of running boards, that could be laid down to form a small bridge when required – an idea pioneered by the French as long ago as 1906. The Silver Ghost was powered by a six-cylinder, dual-ignition engine with a capacity of seven litres but it had a high rate of fuel consumption, around eight miles per gallon.

Of the sixty open-style cars originally ordered it is believed that only about fifteen actually arrived in France. Photographic evidence suggests that the majority of these were Talbots and Wolseleys although many of the latter were soon converted into unarmoured tenders when their springs showed signs of giving way under the strain. Thus it seems reasonable to assume that some of the Rolls-Royces from the first order were in fact completed as turreted cars, while other chassis were ordered direct from the manufacturer or obtained from dealers around the country. The total number of Rolls-Royces armoured in this way is estimated at about eighty.

*37  A brand new Silver Ghost chassis ready to leave the Rolls-Royce works at Derby. The twin rear wheels indicate that it is destined to become an armoured car.*

**38** *The classic First World War armoured car; a Rolls-Royce of No. 2 Squadron RNAS outside the Fire Station in Southwold during training exercises.*

**39** *The turreted version of the Talbot photographed at Wormwood Scrubs. From this angle only the Warland spoked wheels serve to distinguish it from a Rolls-Royce.*

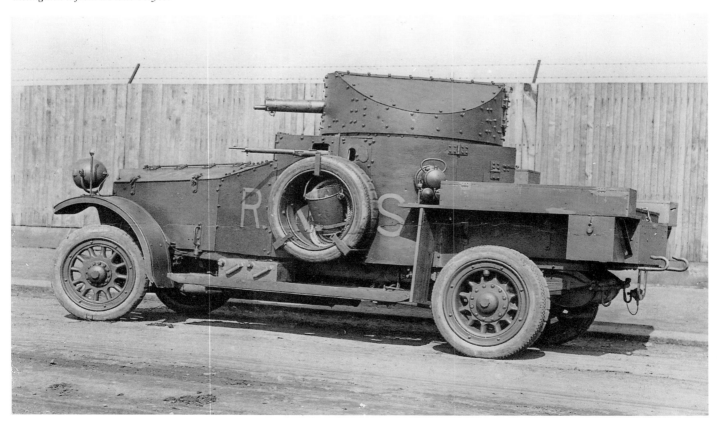

Three turreted cars were ready for delivery by December 1914 and nine more were completed by the New Year. Formed as a squadron of twelve cars, they were sent to East Anglia for training purposes and to be on hand lest the Germans tried to invade the country through that region. Three Talbots were also built to virtually the same design; they are identified by their Warland, artillery-pattern spoked wheels and they too, presumably, were the balance of the order for open-top cars. However the second most popular type of armoured car to see service with the RNAS was the Lanchester. The name is almost forgotten now but it was one of the most remarkable cars of its day.

Frederick Lanchester built his first car in 1895. Unlike his contemporaries, who were generally content to employ horse-drawn carriage techniques for automobile construction, F.W. Lanchester designed his cars to original precepts from the wheels up. By 1914 most of the design work had passed into the capable hands of his younger brother George, and a typical tourer of this period featured a 38 hp, six-cylinder engine, mounted alongside the driver, with a three-speed epicyclic gearbox and cantilever rear springs. In choosing this chassis for armoured car work the Admiralty designers took full advantage of the engine layout to produce a vehicle with a long, sloping bonnet that improved visibility and gave much better ballistic deflection than the conventional bonnets of the Rolls-Royces and Talbots. This novel shape did not allow for the fitting of radiator doors, so horizontal pivoting panels were used instead. The rest of the hull and the turret were virtually identical to those of other makes. About three dozen Lanchesters were completed for the Royal Navy, but they tended to keep themselves apart and in time carved out a legend of their own.

The success of Commander Samson's lorry with the three-pounder gun led to a demand for an armoured version to support the lighter cars in action. Clearly if it was to take the weight of the gun and sufficient armour plate it would need to be a good deal sturdier than the average British three-tonner, and a five-ton chassis was considered ideal. Most lorries of this payload manufactured in Britain were steam wagons, which were clearly unsuitable, but it was a popular size for petrol trucks in the United States. The chassis chosen by the Admiralty was the chain-drive Standard from Detroit, which was marketed in Britain under the trade name of Seabrook. Some thirty chassis were earmarked for conversion and sent to the Portholme Aerodrome Company of Huntingdon where, under the supervision of Lieutenant W.G. Wilson, they were fitted with guns and armour. This was the man who had designed the armoured gun tractor for Armstrong Whitworth in 1906. Latterly he had been working with the Hallford lorry concern in Dartford, where he was co-designer of another armoured car which never saw the light of day. Wilson then joined the RNAS and his connection with the armoured cars at this point is significant since it was the direct cause of his involvement in the invention of the British tank.

The Seabrook armoured lorry was a massive affair. The

*40 A 38 hp Lanchester chassis modified for armoured car work with extra springs and twin rear wheels.*

*41 The wooden mock-up body on a Lanchester chassis shows how the unusual layout suited it well to armoured car design.*

*42 A fully equipped Lanchester; car No. 1 of C Section, 5 Squadron RNACD at Wormwood Scrubs.*

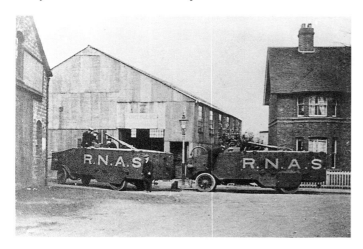

engine was completely protected, with the usual hinged radiator doors at the front. The driving compartment was open at the top, with an ingenious slope-sided head cover which could be moved sideways on rails. This permitted the driver to have his head in the open for normal driving, giving him a good field of vision, but to slide the cover over his head when under fire. It also allowed the cover to be moved out of the way to clear the field of fire when the gun was in action. The three-pounder was mounted on a pedestal in the centre of the main body with full 360° rotation. The sides of the fighting compartment were hinged in two places so that they could be unfolded to give sufficient room for the crew to work the gun when the lorry was in its firing position. Some of the lorries mounted guns fitted with shields while others seem not to have carried them. The rearmost section of the body formed an armoured ammunition container and there were mountings for machine guns at all four corners which could be emplaced for close-in defence as required. A final, typically naval touch was the provision of a staff at the back from which a White Ensign could be flown.

Rigid organization was not a strong feature of the Samson era. His cars may have had a nominal crew of four but the raids were a popular activity and some very undignified squabbles took place if a volunteer looked like being left out. Indeed contemporary photographs seem to suggest that most of these cars went into action heavily overmanned. Once the Admiralty-built cars started to arrive the image of the 'Dunkirk Circus', as the Army liked to call it, was bound to change. The original sixty cars were to have been divided into four fifteen-car squadrons, the Armoured Car Squadrons of the Royal Naval Air Service (Aeroplane Support), to give them their proper title, although it would appear that none of them reached establishment, at least in France. Training was carried out alongside the airmen at Sheerness but in due course the formation moved to London, basing itself at the *Daily Mail* Airship Sheds at Wormwood Scrubs while recruiting was handled by the

RNAS Headquarters at the Crystal Palace. The official title now became the Royal Naval Armoured Car Division which soon amounted to fifteen squadrons of which five were issued with motorcycle machine gun combinations while the rest employed armoured cars. The approved structure of a squadron was three sections, each comprising four armoured cars, one armoured lorry, two supply waggons and eight motorcycles. Section A also included a staff car, Section B a wireless waggon and Section C an ambulance. Squadron headquarters consisted of four motorcycles and one heavy lorry for carrying the unit kit. Squadrons 1,2,3,4,7 and 8 used Rolls-Royces; 5,6 and 15 had Lanchesters while 14 was an oddity with six Rolls-Royces plus the three turreted Talbots and the three original turreted Delaunay-Bellevilles. The missing numbers represented the motorcycle squadrons.

The men were recruited from four centres: London, Liverpool (through the Royal Automobile Club), Derby (through Rolls-Royce Ltd) and Glasgow for what were described as 'Scottish Engineers'. Garage mechanics and chauffeurs were preferred and the Division set very high standards indeed. After an initial period of training at Wormwood Scrubs the squadrons were dispersed to various locations around London – Welwyn, Goring, Henley, Dorking, Abingdon, Warlingham, Oxted and Caterham are mentioned – where they learned to function as an entity and acquire a degree of self-sufficiency. At this time un-armoured Wolseley wagons were used for elementary practical training but, once they were issued with armoured cars, each squadron was despatched for a period of training and anti-invasion duty on the east coast.

Now that the armoured car idea seemed to have caught on and a respectable number of suitable machines were available, commanded and crewed by the right sort of men, opportunities for their use simply evaporated. At least this was true of the front in France, where the expanding trench lines and the rapidly deteriorating terrain of no-man's-land inhibited mobility. There was certainly no point in sending all the squadrons to the Continent although there were plenty of opportunities going begging on other shores. It would mean, of course, that the Admiralty would be pressed to exercise close control over its new arm, but this accorded with their tradition of independent command and suited the character of most of the squadron commanders. In any case there were influential elements within the Admiralty who questioned and vigorously opposed this diversion of effort into land based armoured warfare. Only the firm support of Winston Churchill, appalled at the lack of initiative shown by the War Office, and the evident enthusiasm of the men themselves could stave off the inevitable, so dispersion out of sight, out of mind, was deemed the wisest policy.

There was no intention to abandon the European front altogether, indeed the first unit to move to its operational area was Commander the Duke of Westminster's No.2 Squadron which left Britain for France in March, 1915.

*44 A posed view of a Seabrook armoured lorry with the side panels folded down, the engine and radiator doors open, and a Maxim gun mounted behind the driver's cab.*

*45 Rolls-Royce armoured cars and Talbot tenders of No. 8 Squadron formed up in Southwold.*

*46   Lanchesters of No. 6 Squadron on a training run close by the Duke of Wellington's old home, Stratfield Saye.*

*47   Rolls-Royce armoured cars loading on to a lighter on the first stage of their journey to war.*

They were detailed to work with the cavalry during the British attack from Neuve Chapelle on 10 March but, despite the initial success of this well-planned offensive, the armoured cars were unable to offer any effective help. The contemporary theory that lumped them together with the cavalry was quite correct but only to the extent that the new arm was a mechanical alternative to mounted troops and not a complementary force. Thus, when the initial infantry attack ran out of steam before it broke upon the German defences, the horsemen were pinned down and the cars forced to stay where they were. Instructions for the employment of armoured cars at this time were rudimentary in the extreme. A set of *Orders and Instructions* for the armoured cars, issued on 1 January 1915, simply stated that the cars should work in pairs, accompanied by a lorry containing eight or twelve cyclists and their machines. The cyclists would scout ahead and fall back upon the armoured cars if they found the enemy. The cars would then move up to drive out the opposition and the advance would continue. Each car, it stated, should carry a quantity of rifle grenades which were considered to be the best possible antidote to

enemy armoured cars. The rest of the book was little more than a catalogue of crimes which the reader was adjured not to commit.

Four more squadrons crossed the Channel in April. No.5 (Lanchester), No.8 (Rolls-Royce), No.15 (Lanchester) and the three armoured Seabrooks only of No.6. The cars from squadrons 5 and 8 went into reserve at Dunkirk while their Seabrooks went to the front. The armoured lorries were far too heavy to exploit their mobility to any extent in the prevailing conditions, the merest ditch or soft patch of ground had to be bridged with planks before the vehicle tried to move across or it was bound to break a spring or sink up to its axles in the mire. The guns were employed simply for their nuisance value, reversing into prepared positions at the front after dark to carry out a pre-arranged shoot and then make a smart getaway before daylight could reveal them to the Germans. A counter barrage always fell on their positions next morning and any lorry that was bogged or broken down would be wiped out. Just such an accident caused the death of the Wimbledon champion Anthony Wilding. That they achieved some success is evident from the fact that the Commander-in-Chief in

*48   Another Davis cartoon gives the Seabrook armoured lorry one quality it never did have – speed.*

*49   A War Artist's somewhat imaginative view of two Seabrooks during a nightime shoot.*

France, Sir John French, applied to the Admiralty for more. All the remaining squadrons lost their Seabrooks which were formed into four new squadrons, Nos 16 to 19, of six armoured lorries apiece, and Squadrons 16 and 17 went out to France in May.

Squadron 15 was diverted to work with the Belgians who were mainly equipped with open-topped Minerva armoured cars, although it would appear that the Belgian army obtained some Lanchesters as well. Commanding the squadron was the Norfolk MP Oliver Locker-Lampson, who saw in this glamourous role a means to fight for his country and enhance his political stature at the same time. A man of more than modest means, he was able partly to fund the squadron from his personal fortune, and supply the balance from a financial reserve accumulated by the Ulster Volunteer Force during the heady Home Rule days of 1912. The Belgians are aggressive and daring motorists at the best of times, and given armoured cars and machine guns they became positive demons, but even they could not achieve the impossible and, as the period of mobile warfare came to an end they and their British allies found fewer and fewer opportunities to use their cars to the best advantage.

If events in France did not augur well for the future of wheeled armoured warfare, conditions elsewhere looked much more inviting. Colonial ambitions, rekindled by the war, provided an excellent opportunity for expansion, particulary in Africa. South African forces, under the Boer veteran Botha, were clearing German South West Africa (Namibia), Togoland and the Cameroons. The Rolls-Royces of No.1 Squadron RNACD sailed from England in March 1915 to assist them. At this time the Dark Continent was hardly opened up to motor vehicles outside settled areas, and conditions for the employment of armoured vehicles seemed poor, to say the least. These cars were fitted with ordinary pneumatic tyres which did not stand up well to the conditions and, operationally, they were tied closely to the railway which in any case was the main axis of advance. Shortly after their arrival by rail from the landing

*50 Camouflaged Lanchesters in Belgian service. The cars are thought to have been on loan from No. 15 Squadron.*

point at Walvis Bay they fought a successful action in defence of the main base camp at Trekkopje but, after that, it was largely a matter of crashing about in the undergrowth or being manhandled over rocky outcrops. By June 1915 Botha's advance had carried him into a dense jungle region that was no place for armoured cars. No.1 Squadron was ordered home, minus four of its cars which were despatched to East Africa.

*51 A Rolls-Royce is swung down from the deck of a transport during the landings at Walvis Bay, German South West Africa.*

*52 From the transport the cars were towed ashore on a lighter by a small tugboat.*

*53 Armoured Cars (Rolls-Royce) of No.1 Squadron in the bush near Serengeti, German East Africa.*

54 *One of the special dugouts on Cape Helles, Gallipoli, where cars of Nos 3 and 4 Squadrons spent most of their time.*

55 *A Rolls-Royce of No. 8 Squadron in the New Forest after the unit's return from France in 1915.*

The Rolls-Royces and possibly one Seabrook from Nos 3 and 4 Squadrons also left England in March 1915, bound for Gallipoli. Once again the terrain of this sparsely inhabited peninsula proved to be unsuitable for motorised warfare. Four cars were brought ashore and parked in specially prepared dugouts on Cape Helles but the remainder stayed on board the transports while their crews fought as dismounted machine gun teams. Lieutenant-Commander Boothby, commanding No.4 Squadron, was killed during the landings but the CO of No.3 Squadron, Lieutenant-Commander Josiah Wedgwood, found few opportunities of using the cars that were ashore. They tried fitting grapnels, on long poles, to the rear of each car, to reverse up to the Turkish wire and tear it away, but this was not the kind of work that armoured cars were designed for. Before the end of June it was clear that the armoured cars could be better employed elsewhere so those that remained aboard ship were carried on to Egypt, to be joined by the four from Cape Helles in August.

Three squadrons – No.6 (Lanchester), No.7 (Rolls-Royce) and the composite No.14 (Rolls-Royce, Talbot and Delaunay-Belleville) – remained in Britain on anti-invasion duty. The threat may not have been taken seriously at the War Office by this time but, to the population on the east coast, especially after the German bombardment of Hartlepool and Scarborough, it was real enough and the sight of the sleek grey armoured cars, with their jaunty naval crews, must have done a lot to stiffen morale.

Meanwhile in France, apart from the Seabrooks, the armoured cars found little to do. The German attack in April, known as Second Ypres, involved No.2 Squadron to a limited extent but the remainder whiled away the time at Dunkirk. In Belgium 15 Squadron faced an equally bleak future and Locker-Lampson saw the prospect of independent command slipping away from him and with it, perhaps, future electoral success. It was the Belgians who provided him with an answer. King Albert was inordinately proud of his Corps of Cannon and Machine Gun Cars, which was also liable to be disbanded if it could find nowhere to fight, so he offered its services to the Russians. This was gratefully accepted and it prompted Locker-Lampson to float the same idea. With strong support from the Czar and his government the case was put to the Admiralty which, caught at a difficult time, was forced to agree. Apart from some special units that were being retained for specific reasons, the Navy was busily engaged in handing armoured cars over to the Army at this time, and those men who did not wish to change services because it involved a drop in pay, or to change to another branch of the Senior Service from that for which they had volunteered, could thus be usefully accommodated. In order to make the contribution more worthwhile it was decided to amalgamate the three Lanchester squadrons into a division and add a heavy support unit drawn from the Seabrook squadron (No.17) that had worked with 15 Squadron in Belgium.

56 A group that includes a Russian officer, alongside a Pierce-Arrow armoured lorry in the United Kingdom.

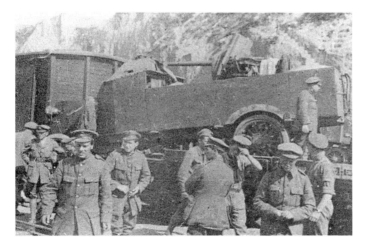

57 The hybrid armoured lorry 'Ulster' – Seabrook body on a Pierce-Arrow chassis – in trouble on a Russian train.

58 This Pierce-Arrow appears to be towing another small gun.

The composition of the Russian Armoured Car Division, RNAS, as it was known to the Admiralty, therefore consisted of some three dozen Lanchester armoured cars supported by three armoured Pierce-Arrow lorries. The Pierce-Arrow was a top quality truck manufactured in the United States and the five-ton version was chosen for conversion into gun lorries. It was already in service with the Royal Navy as a conventional lorry and with the Royal Marines as an armoured anti-aircraft wagon, having proved itself much more robust than the Seabrook and less troublesome in service since it did not feature the unpopular chain final drive. The three armoured lorries were given the names Ulster, Londonderry and Mountjoy, revealing the Irish connection to those in the know, and Ulster was a most interesting vehicle since, to all outward appearances it was a Seabrook. However the registration number, OA-2349, and the shaft-drive rear axle indicate that it was a Pierce Arrow chassis mounting the body and armament of a Seabrook. The other two lorries were made to an original design by the firm of W.G. Allen & Sons of Tipton, Staffordshire with armoured bonnets that seem to have derived from the anti-aircraft lorries, half-width drivers' cabs and an enormous turret amidships, mounting a three-pounder gun. The shape revealed that the turret had evolved from the pattern designed for the Rolls-Royce and Lanchester cars. It had a traverse of about 300°, being masked for the rest of the arc by the cab. The gun protruded from an oval opening at the front and a sliding door was provided at the back. Behind the turret were two wooden locker-cum-seats, plated over for extra protection.

The lorries were armoured to about 9 mm standard, giving an all-up weight of about nine tons which, in service, caused a great deal of trouble. One lorry was modified while the unit was in Russia, the turret being taken off and the gun retained on an open mounting with limited traverse. The gap in each side was filled by sheet-metal plates which restricted the movement of the guncrew but at least helped to reduce the weight. Two more turreted models, armoured to only 5 mm standard, are thought to have been supplied later on.

59 The modified, turretless Pierce-Arrow with a very mixed crew in Galicia.

**60** A Lanchester armoured car, followed by a Lanchester tender head a convoy across the endless Russian plains.

**61** The Rolls-Royce armoured car that accompanied Locker-Lampson's force to Russia. It is fitted with tyre chains for the snow and special shields to protect the barrel of the machine-gun, a favourite Russian modification.

**62** A Russian-built armoured car on a Fiat chassis, probably on loan to the Russian Armoured Car Division. Notice in the background the discarded turret of a Pierce-Arrow.

**63** A Ford T armoured car in the works yard at Tipton prior to the mounting of a machine gun.

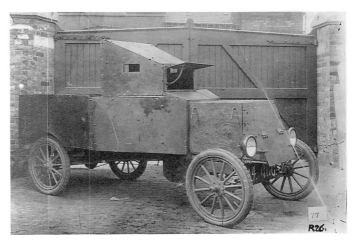

**64** A rear view of an armoured Ford in Russia with the machine gun in place.

**65** A Fiat 15 ter lorry with the body from an armoured Ford in the back and panels of armour from a Lanchester fitted to the cab.

66 *A special carriage for a 3-pdr gun, towed by a Rolls-Royce. Built at Barlby Road it was probably too heavy for service.*

The exploits of Locker-Lampson's Division have already filled a book★ so there is no need, or space, to repeat them here. Suffice it to say that after arriving in Russia in January 1916 they fought a lone and magnificent war, from the Caucasus to Roumania and from Galicia to the Ukraine, against Austrians and Turks, atrocious conditions and, latterly, hostile Russian Bolsheviks whose burgeoning revolution finally brought their activities to an end. Although they were financed and supplied by the Russian government, the vast distances and the notorious inefficiency of the Czarist system demanded a considerable degree of self-sufficiency on the part of the Britons. In addition to the armoured vehicles they took with them a substantial fleet of lorries, ambulances and mobile workshops on Pierce-Arrow and Austin chassis along with motorcycles and Lanchester staff cars and light tenders. Locker-Lampson took his own Rolls-Royce touring car with him and there was a single Rolls-Royce armoured car which proved to be so much stronger than the Lanchesters that there was a move, at one stage, to have all the armoured cars replaced by Rolls-Royces, although this proved to be impossible. Armoured cars on Austin, Fiat and other chassis were occasionally borrowed from Russian stocks while, by December 1916,

★'*The Czar's British Squadron*' by Perrett and Lord, Kimber, 1981.

the unit was strengthened with the arrival of some half-dozen light armoured cars on Ford Model T chassis. These cars were built to a design worked out by Chief Petty Officer L. Gutteridge at the unit's home base at Newport, Monmouthshire and they, too, were assembled in Tipton.

The Fords were produced in answer to a call for lighter armoured vehicles with a better ground clearance, following the experience of the first campaign season. Armoured all over with a narrow, one-man cab for the driver and an open, round-backed tray at the rear, each mounted a Vickers machine gun on its tripod, clipped to the floor for rapid dismounting. In Russia one car was altered to carry a Lewis gun in a shorter body while the hull of another was mounted on the back of a Fiat lorry which had extra panels of armour around the cab.

In addition to the Headquarters at Wormwood Scrubs, the RNACD had a repair and maintenance depot nearby at the Clement-Talbot Company works in Barlby Road, North Kensington. Here about twenty ratings from No. 14 Squadron, under Lieutenant-Commander McGrath, carried out a number of experiments in addition to their normal repair work. Two early projects involved Rolls-Royce cars; one was equipped with a strong towbar to which was fitted a three-pounder gun on a very substantial steel carriage. Of riveted construction, with a large shield and solid-tyred disc wheels, it looked most impressive. No doubt it derived from Samson's improvised version but, although cars were later seen in France towing similar home-made concoctions there is no evidence to indicate that the London gun ever went out there. In all probability it was much too heavy to tow. Another Rolls was modified to undertake fire support work in an altogether more drastic way. The turret was removed and a big Vickers one-pounder Pom-Pom was mounted in the fighting compartment. The gun had all-round traverse and a sizeable shield but was so big that the gunner had to fire the weapon from outside, standing in the rear section to aim forward or balancing on the running board when the gun was trained aft. This was clearly unsatisfactory and, as far as is known, the car never left Britain in this form.

*67 Lightweight 3-pdr gun carriages were used in France. The Rolls-Royce that is towing this one has extra plating in the rear.*

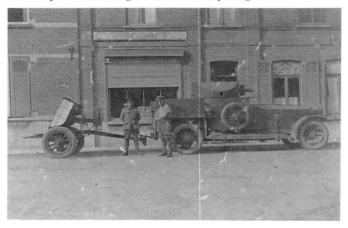

*68 Family Day at the RNAS Depot at Barlby Road and a photograph with the unique Rolls-Royce Pom-Pom car.*

The problems of operating armoured cars in desert conditions had hardly been grasped before the Royal Navy surrendered its equipment to the Army, but these were in the air, and one aspect was considered at Barlby Road. It was argued that heavy cars would soon become bogged down in soft sand and lose traction, so an alternative means of propulsion was devised. An armoured car was built, as a mock-up, on a Sizaire-Berwick chassis and fitted with a 110 hp Sunbeam aircraft engine at the back, driving a four-bladed airscrew which, it was hoped, would virtually blow the car along if the wheels became stuck. Naturally this extra engine and the massive rear-facing propellor took up a good deal of chassis space which, in turn, placed serious limitations on the size and shape of the fighting compartment. A turret was obviously out of the question so, behind the bonnet, a slope-fronted cab was built in mild steel with space for a driver on the right and alongside him a gunner, who operated a forward-firing Maxim. The car was constructed at the Sizaire-Berwick works but it was never developed beyond the prototype stage. For one thing it was soon discovered that armoured cars were not so helpless in the desert as some people had imagined and, in any case, a general shortage of aircraft engines for the flying services precluded their being used as auxiliary power units for armoured vehicles in secondary theatres of war.

The number of men under McGrath steadily increased as the workload grew and their experimental work took on a new significance. The best armoured cars in France were quite incapable of moving off the roads, and even these were deteriorating rapidly in the battle zone. They could hardly force their way through heavy wire entanglements and they certainly could not cross trenches. If the concept of armoured warfare was to survive on the Western Front then clearly a new means had to be found to enable it to overcome these conditions and if a way was to be found then the naval armoured car men were the ones to do it. Their enthusiasm and faith in the efficacy of mechanized fighting gave them the incentive and their familiarity with complex machinery provided the means. There was no shortage of ideas and, before long, a series of strange and very secret experiments were being carried out behind the high fence that surrounded the Talbot Works. In due course a new squadron, number 20, was formed to concentrate on this work while the Admiralty set up a Landships Committee to examine the various proposals. The results of this move have already been explained in a companion volume* but one particular experiment can be repeated here. This took place in the summer of 1915 when the body of one of the original Delaunay-Belleville armoured cars of No. 14 Squadron, with its turret removed, was mounted onto the frame of a small, tracklaying Killen-Strait tractor. It was tested briefly in this form and, improvisation though it was, deserves to be recorded as the first armoured, tracklaying vehicle ever built; the true forerunner of the tank.

*'Landships, British Tanks in the First World War' Fletcher, HMSO 1984.

What had begun almost as a private venture had now grown into a large independent organization, albeit one that was scattered over many thousands of miles. It was serving a useful purpose, there was no doubt about that, but its activities had a lot more to do with the Army than the Royal Navy, and there were influential members of the Admiralty who could see no sense in it at all. While Winston Churchill kept his hand on the helm there was little that could be done to change things but when he fell from favour over the Gallipoli debâcle the situation changed. Pressure on manpower and resources were other reasons for disbanding the RNACD but there were all kinds of complications. Negotiations with the War Office resulted, in August 1915, in the transfer of most of the armoured cars to the Army, although the men who manned them were not always inclined to follow suit. Whether the Army wanted the cars at this stage is debatable. They had proved their worth in every region except where it mattered most, in France, but it was a logical step and the benefits were appreciated in due course.

The transfer did not take place overnight; it was October before some units changed hands while others were subject to special dispensations. Locker-Lampson's force in Russia was so far out of reach that it hardly mattered at all who was controlling it and Churchill's successor at the Admiralty, the ex-Prime Minister A. J. Balfour, was persuaded to retain 20 Squadron under naval command on account of the important work it was doing. Indeed this squadron remained responsible for testing and delivering tanks right up to the end of the war. The section in East Africa was also retained for the time being, simply because the Army had no trained men to take over and the work it was doing was vital.

69  *The Sizaire-Berwick 'Wind-wagon' winds up its aero engine. The machine gun would occupy the hole in the cab front to the left of the driver.*

*70 & 70a   A Scottish Motor Traction 'Lothian' lorry, probably ex-Edinburgh Fire Service and an equally rare Durham Churchill (below) that seems to have started life as a charabanc, temporarily rigged up as gun lorries. The location is believed to be the Rosyth Naval Dockyard on the Forth.*

# CHAPTER 3

# In the Army Now

By the autumn of 1915 the War Office found itself the proud, if reluctant, owner of a fleet of armoured vehicles wished upon it by the Admiralty. The first reaction, at least in respect of those units stationed close to home, was to withdraw all of them to storage areas and try to forget about them. Some of the Rolls-Royces were even stripped of their armour and converted into staff cars or light trucks. Other cars were loaned to Territorial Cyclist Battalions for internal security work but those that had gone out to Africa and the Middle East were left alone for the present since they were doing useful work and there appeared to be little point in disturbing them.

However it would be wrong to suggest that the Army was totally devoid of imagination and that it had not acquired some armoured cars of its own. Some Yeomanry Regiments

of the Territorial Army, upon mobilization, had allowed their enthusiasm to get the better of them. Their officers, presumably inspired by the initiative shown by the Royal Navy and the continental allies, sometimes raised funds to provide a couple of armoured cars although design was very much a matter of personal preference. The Westmorland and Cumberland Yeomanry was one of the first regiments thus affected and two cars were built on Italian-made Issotta-Fraschini chassis by the Guy Lewin Company in London. One was relatively conventional, with hinged radiator doors at the front, no extra protection for the bonnet and a box-shaped armoured hull with a sloping front face. A tiny turret was fitted at one stage but there is no evidence of a fixed armament. The other car was most unusual. The hull was like some huge, misshapen lozenge

*71 Checking the tyres on one of the Westmorland and Cumberland Yeomanry's Isotta-Fraschinis.*

72  *Bodywork by Guy Lewin to a design by the Westmorland and Cumberland Yeomanry, the other Isotta-Fraschini was an ugly brute.*

with a long sloping nose and sharp, pointed tail. Long, narrow rifle-slits, protected by sliding covers, were fitted all around the hull while a double-flap hatch was provided in the roof with a smaller one just ahead of it housing a spotlight.

The 2nd King Edward's Horse was a regiment raised from colonial volunteers in London. It employed the coachbuilders Barker and Co. to fit an armoured hull onto a 25 hp Talbot chassis. The result was a large, turreted car of conventional layout but built entirely from flat panels, causing the turret to look out of all proportion with the hull. A dummy machine gun was fitted for show and KT studded tyres were used on the front wheels, which were supposed to prevent skidding. Another car, almost certainly from the same builders, was a very smart Rolls-Royce which was clearly based on the Admiralty's turreted design. Again, since no curved plates were used it was quite distinctive but the turret was bevelled at the top and consequently not so overpowering. There is no direct evidence to connect it with the 2nd KEH and the officer posing alongside it appears to belong to a Scottish regiment.

In due course, as the war put more and more pressure on reserves of manpower these enthusiastic regiments were absorbed and lost their identities. Their records are

accordingly scanty at best so the fate of the cars remains a mystery. It seems unlikely that they ever accompanied the troops abroad and in all probability their greatest asset was as an aid to recruiting.

The activities of the naval armoured cars even caused a small stir at the War Office. Early in 1915 Lord Kitchener approached Commodore Sueter for some advice on armoured car construction and a RNAS officer, Flight Commander T.G. Hetherington, was interviewed by Kitchener and other senior officers before being asked to visit the Woolwich Arsenal to report on what they were up to. Hetherington was shown a fully armoured lorry built on to the chassis of an AEC bus. Since they had not bothered to consult the Navy on the subject, the designers at Woolwich had chosen to use armour so thin that it would not even stop a rifle bullet at 100 yards range. Although the engine, cab and body were completely covered there was no turret and no fixed mountings for weapons, just a series of large, sliding shutters all round the body and in the front of the cab. Hetherington's comments were not very complimentary but it seems to have impressed Kitchener that such a young man should be so well informed on the subject. The vehicle was never sent abroad for active service but seems to have spent its time patrolling the South Coast;

73    A Barker bodied Talbot of the 2nd King Edward's Horse.

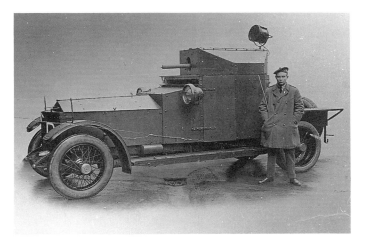

74    The identity of the regiment that owned this handsome Rolls-Royce, also by Barkers, is unknown.

76    The tiny AC armoured car, dwarfed by its enormous turret, is seen here during War Office trials in the Aldershot area.

75    The first official War Office design for an armoured car was built at Woolwich Arsenal on a B type bus chassis. Condemned by an Admiralty expert for its thin armour it never left the country.

it was photographed later in Ramsgate with some of the armour removed, including the radiator cover, which suggests that it had cooling problems. Another War Office-inspired armoured car was the AC, which was a complete contrast to the bus. Built by Autocarriers Ltd. of Thames Ditton, Surrey, the AC was one of a range of light motorcars that were gaining popularity at the time. It was powered by an 1100 cc Fivet engine driving through a three speed gearbox built into the rear axle. Curved armoured doors shielded the radiator and the fighting compartment consisted of a large circular shield with a single machine gun port, resting on top of the hull. This gave the car a particularly top-heavy look and, despite the fact that the suspension had been almost totally rebuilt to cope with the weight, it seems that the chassis was altogether too light to carry the load. Photographs show the car with as many as five men on board although a crew of three would appear to have been more than enough. It was tested at Aldershot and presumably rejected, since no more was heard of it.

An altogether more professional type of armoured car was built in 1915 by Vickers Ltd through their Wolseley subsidiary, using that firm's 30 cwt model CP lorry chassis. Two were made to the order of the London Mounted Brigade using funds collected by the Lord Mayor of London. Bonnet and hull were well armoured in contemporary fashion while the turret was an original design. It took the form of a low drum, probably open at the top but with a raised central section that housed the machine gun and gunner. Steel discs were fitted over the wheel spokes and it is believed to have been the first time this was done on a wartime British armoured car although it was by no means a new idea. Another car of this type is said to have been built for the War Office but it is unlikely that any of them went overseas.

Despite the global nature of the First World War it was still a time when an enterprising adventurer could raise what amounted to a small private army, provided he could afford it. Such a man was Sir John Willoughby, a veteran of the Jameson Raid with wide interests in Africa. Early in 1915 he ordered four armoured lorries from Leyland Motors and then offered them, complete with crews and support vehicles, to the War Office for service in East Africa under his command. The armoured cars were quite large, being on the firm's three ton Subsidy Type chassis, and naturally quite heavy. They were well armoured with a centrally-mounted turret, disc wheels and hinged radiator louvres. A door was provided in the right side of the body so that both unditching channels were stowed on the left. There was a machine gun mounted in the turret and another in the rear of the body along with a duplicate steering position for driving in reverse. Since they were designed to operate in a region where roads were poor, if they existed at all, special attention was paid to the underside of the chassis, where as many fittings as possible were tucked safely out of sight to improve ground clearance. Each car carried a crew of six and the unit was raised at Bisley. The

78  Sir John Willoughby strikes a nonchalant pose in front of one of his armoured Leylands outside the works. Notice the spotlight and the little semaphore signalling device on top of the cab.

79  It was another story when the Leylands got to East Africa. The narrow wheels cut deep ruts in the primitive roads and the fancy fittings were soon dispensed with.

77  Wolseley Motors was part of the Vickers group in 1915 when the latter firm fitted an armoured body to this Wolseley CP 30 cwt chassis.

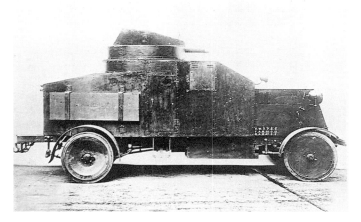

36

80 *The lower car, FX119, is certainly Mr Ismay's Mercedes armoured by Vickers-Wolseley. The top one may be the same car in an earlier guise.*

Fast Armoured Car Fitted with Colt Automatic Gun.

Fast Armoured Car with Revolving Turret and Machine Gun.

War Office must have thought that it was something it was in desperate need of since they gave way to Willoughby's demand that his company be known as No.1 (Willoughby's) Armoured Motor Battery, notwithstanding the existence of another battery with the same numerical designation that was operating in Egypt. On their own books, however, it appeared more prosaically as 322 Company, Army Service Corps.

The Leylands arrived in East Africa in March 1916, along with two Rolls-Royce batteries. It was soon discovered that they were much too heavy for the terrain and liable to sink into the mud with the least provocation. Wide flanges were added to the wheels in an effort to cure this and many non-essential items were removed in order to reduce the weight but this failed to make very much difference. Later in the year the battery moved to Egypt where the Army Service Corps tried to take it over since it was, technically, on their books. Willoughby resigned in protest while the Leylands were forwarded to Mesopotamia to be converted, later, into anti-aircraft lorries when their armour was removed.

Mr J.H. Ismay of Iwerne Minster, Dorset was another private citizen who decided to supply his regiment with an armoured car. He was associated with two local yeomanry regiments and the car he offered for conversion was probably his own vehicle, a 45 hp Mercedes tourer. Two photographs exist of armoured Mercedes and it is tempting to assume that they show two manifestations of the same car. The first is turretless, open at the top and mounting a Colt machine gun. The second is certainly Ismay's. It carries a Dorset registration and is known to have been armoured by the Wolseley Company in 1916. The front end is virtually identical to the earlier car but it sports a turret, not unlike that fitted to the armoured Wolseley built for the Lord Mayor of London. Although good armoured cars were at a premium in 1916 there was obviously little to be gained by adding all manner of odd makes and models to a fleet since it would frustrate and confuse the repair facilities to a ridiculous degree. It is not surprising, therefore, to discover that no record exists of this car ever entering service.

The transfer of armoured cars from the Royal Naval Air Service was a slow, complicated and frustrating business. The cars now came under the Machine Gun Corps (Motors), organized into four-car batteries known variously as Armoured Motor Batteries (AMBs), Light Armoured Batteries (LABs), Light Armoured Car Batteries (LACBs) and finally as Light Armoured Motor Batteries (LAMBs). Initially all the cars in France returned to Britain and the first to leave again were Nos.1, 2 and 3 AMB which had previously been the Duke of Westminster's No.2 Squadron. They went back to France in October 1915 where they found little to do and then moved on to Egypt in December where a most exciting career awaited them. In March 1916 three more units, 7, 8 and 9 LAB, arrived in France. 7 LAB had five Rolls-Royce cars while the others had four each. They were attached to the cavalry and employed mostly on liaison work but generally, when they did try to get into action, as on the Somme in July, they ended up getting bogged down in the mud. By the autumn of 1916 a wind of change was blowing through the Army in France; the first tanks had arrived. Despite their common ancestry no attempt was made to co-ordinate the activities of these two armoured arms. They operated in the same area for a while during the Battle of Arras in April 1917, but they might as well have been fighting in different wars. The tanks did reasonably well but were far better suited to the conditions, while the armoured cars spent most of their time hanging about in the wings.

By the time of Arras the dozen or so cars in France had undergone some modifications. Pivoting hooks had been added to the front of each machine to enable it to drag away barbed wire and some were again being fitted with towbars to haul light guns. A month earlier some of the cars had been used to follow up the German retreat to the Hindenburg Line and this produced some interesting lessons. Fighting in village streets, they discovered that enemy troops in the upper storeys of buildings forced the

81    A Rolls-Royce of the Machine Gun Corps (Motors) near
Abbeville in 1916. The gun has been fitted with an armoured jacket and
a small shield.

82    An MGC Rolls-Royce surveys the distant trenches which bar its
way into enemy territory.

83    If an armoured car ventured off the road in the shell-torn
landscape near the front it soon got bogged down and became an easy
target for enemy artillery.

commander to stay closed down inside his turret, thus robbing him of any chance to observe and direct his crew. Secondly the Germans were developing armour-piercing ammunition to defeat the tanks and this had a disastrous effect on lightly-armoured cars. In order to counter these problems all the cars were withdrawn to their base at Calais and fitted with armoured lookout cupolas of various patterns on top of the turret. As an antidote to the armour-piercing bullet the cars were then clad in panels of a thick lightweight substance called Uralite, a fireproof, mineral-based building material, which effectively slowed down the bullet and prevented penetration. Most cars were then camouflage painted in a random three-tone colour scheme.

The Battle of Cambrai, which began on 20 November 1917, finally vindicated those who had pinned their faith on the tank. Planned by the Tank Corps as a glorified raid, it was treated at GHQ as a full scale battle intended to smash the Hindenburg Line, and the cavalry was massed to exploit the breakout. In the event they never got the chance; at the first sign of an enemy machine gun the mounted arm was

driven to take cover. When one considers what a small force of armoured cavalry, mounted in fast-moving cars, could have achieved on this dry, undamaged downland, the inability of the British High Command to appreciate the full potential of armoured warfare becomes painfully evident. However at this crucial time the opportunity was lost since the three Rolls-Royce batteries were on their way to the Middle East. It would be over four months before British armoured cars returned to the Western Front, and three more before they finally saw action alongside the tanks which they had helped to spawn.

Egypt in 1915 was the hub of the war effort in the Near East. From here units could strike westwards into the Sahara Desert to deal with dissident tribes goaded into action by the Turks, or northwards into Gaza to confront the Turkish army itself. To chronicle all the armoured car units involved would be tedious in the extreme since the batteries were small organizations which came and went, exchanging cars and personnel with monotonous regularity.

The first armoured cars to arrive in Egypt were the balance of squadrons 3 and 4 which were not sent ashore on

*84 Two camouflaged Rolls-Royces near Arras in April 1917. Both cars have cupolas added to their turrets, a cladding of Uralite over vital areas and a hook at the front to rip down barbed wire.*

85 *The Duke of Westminster 'Bend Or' (on the right) poses with two fellow officers at Mersah Matruh.*

Gallipoli. They were used to form an Emergency Squadron to patrol the Egyptian border from their base at Alexandria, which they did until January 1916, when the three batteries under the Duke of Westminster arrived in the area. The Emergency Squadron was manned by the RNAS pending the training of Army personnel and, when its period of service was over, the cars were used to form Nos 11 and 12 LAMB. Meanwhile the Duke of Westminster, now serving as a Major in the Cheshire Yeomanry, took his cars by sea to Mersah Matruh in order to harry the Senussi. They were a warlike Arab religious sect goaded into action by the Turks to tie down as many British troops as possible. The Duke's armoured cars took part in the recapture of Sollum where they heard of the fate of the crew of the British steamer Tara which had been sunk off the African Coast by gunfire from a U-Boat. It was believed at home that these men were all lost but in fact they had reached the shore in boats, only to be captured by the Sennussi and marched away into the desert. A rescue plan was formulated at once, involving a fleet of Ford cars, escorted by Rolls-Royces, which arrived at the enemy encampment at dawn after an overnight drive. Faced with this kind of opposition the Arabs fled, leaving their captives behind.

86 *Anzac soldiers pose in and around a Rolls-Royce in the Western Desert. This car has had the armour removed from the top of the bonnet and turret as a concession to the heat.*

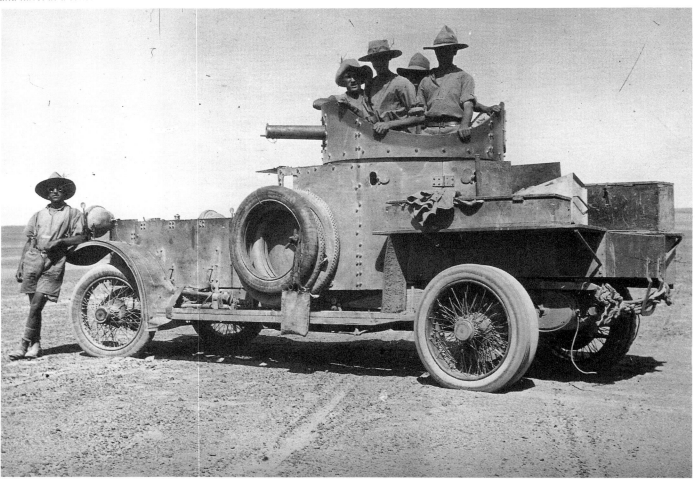

British control of Egypt in 1914 did not meet with the universal approval of the inhabitants so a certain amount of internal security work was necessary, and armoured cars were ideal in this respect. However, only a few were available and at least one had to be built locally. Known as the 'Terror' it was based in Cairo and sometimes referred to as the 'Mother of the Cairo Fleet'. The chassis was a chain-drive Commer, so old that it was described as 'ancient' by the magazine *Autocar* in 1916! It was a massive vehicle with a long armoured bonnet and even longer hull surmounted by two turrets which had sun shields on top. Its progress was so slow and stately that it could hardly be

expected to turn out to a trouble spot in time to do any good and the best that could be hoped for, according to one contemporary report, was that it would impress the natives.

The very nature of the desert fighting, so unlike that on the Western Front, did not really call for all-round armour protection. In addition, the climate made conditions inside the enclosed cars intolerable, so a number of modifications were introduced. The simplest and most common was to remove the top plates of the turret, although some cars were seen without turrets at all and one at least was given a longer armoured hull and no turret. Unarmoured cars also appeared, almost always Rolls-Royces which may have been

*87 'The Terror' a massive armoured chain-drive Commer of uncertain vintage that prowled around Cairo, keeping the peace.*

*88 This Rolls-Royce, photographed in the Sudan, has no turret at all, just a large shield for the machine gun.*

*89 This turretless Rolls-Royce had extra armour added to the rear end of the hull, which is probably why it has got itself bogged down in the sand.*

90 Some Rolls-Royce armoured cars were converted back to tenders with a machine gun mounted at the back. Notice how the armoured Rolls alongside has cooling louvres cut into the top of the bonnet.

91 The original, pre-1916 version, of the Ford T had an angular brass radiator, surmounted in this case by a large whistle. Nominally the property of a Light Car Patrol it is being used here on an unofficial shooting trip near Sollum.

92 The later Model Ford T had a different style of radiator. This LCP vehicle also mounts a Lewis gun for more serious shooting.

armoured once or started life as staff cars. They usually mounted a machine gun at the rear. In a few cases the armoured bonnet only was retained while the rest of the body was improvised from wood, indeed the variations appear to be endless.

All the same, the Rolls-Royce was a heavy car in any form and rather low-slung, so that choice of ground was always an important factor when travelling in the desert. Since mobility was more important than armour in this region it was argued that a lighter car, with good ground clearance, might prove more effective. The obvious choice lay at the other end of the social scale from the Rolls-Royce, the Model T Ford, and before long large numbers of these cars, which were already serving as light trucks all over the Middle East, were organised into Light Car Patrols, for long-range raiding and desert patrols. A patrol comprised five Fords, each mounting a Lewis gun, and a supply tender. Their most important operation in Egypt was the raid against the Sennussi at Siwa Oasis in 1917. Supported by the Rolls-Royces of Nos 1 and 3 AMB, they undertook a 300-mile round trip from Sollum and caught a large enemy force at their desert base. An effective combination of surprise, mobility and automatic firepower finally broke the Sennussi for good.

Another offshoot from the pool of ex-RNAS cars in Egypt was the Hedjaz Armoured Car Section of three Rolls-Royce armoureds and two tenders which operated alongside the irregular forces inspired and guided by T.E. Lawrence. His fame as Lawrence of Arabia and the evocative image he presented in Arabian robes, mounted on a camel and surrounded by his colourful bodyguard, should not obscure the fact that he often employed British specialists and equipment. Indeed he was always ready to mount a long-range raid entirely with British troops on motorized mounts such as that against the Amman railway bridge in September 1918. Another unit that served with the Hedjaz section deserves notice; the 10th Motor Section, Royal Field Artillery, was composed of half a dozen Talbot wagons, two of which carried light Indian Army pattern mountain howitzers. Lawrence's force was supplemented by two more armoured cars of No.1 LACB in May 1918 and the cars earned his undying respect for their reliability in the most trying conditions. Speaking of an accident which damaged a rear spring on an overloaded tender Lawrence, in his 'Seven Pillars of Wisdom', says that it was the first such failure in eighteen months' service; that a Rolls in the desert was above rubies. What better testimonial could any manufacture desire?

Apart from these diversions the most important task allotted to the British and Commonwealth troops in Egypt was the protection of the Suez Canal. As long as Gallipoli and the setback in Mesopotamia tied up so many men, a defensive posture was the only option, but the situation changed early in 1916 with the appointment of Sir Archibald Murray to the command of the newly formed Egyptian Expeditionary Force. A slow but deliberate advance, with little scope for armoured action, brought the Allied troops to Gaza where they were halted by two successive defeats and remained held up until the midsummer of 1917 when Sir Edmund Allenby took over. His appointment coincided with a new political significance in the area which authorized considerable reinforcements and, on the Turkish side, the arrival of the German General von Falkenhayn. He brought with him a special German Asian Corps and a body of advisers to breathe new life into the wilting Turkish army with an offensive codenamed *Yilderim* – lightning – or, as the Germans might have it, *Blitzkrieg*.

German attitudes failed to endear them to the Turks and in any event, it was the British who struck first. Allenby's Third Gaza Battle in October 1917, which involved a few tanks, finally broke the stalemate and initiated a pursuit which ended, twelve months later near Aleppo, with the end of the war against Turkey. Armoured cars and Light Car Patrols played a significant part in many actions during that year, graduating from reconnaissance missions and raids to significant outflanking manoeuvres in larger battles. One of the most intersting armoured car actions of the period occured shortly before the end of the war, some miles south of Aleppo, when a group of Rolls-Royces got into a running fight with an armoured car and lorries armed with machine guns, probably under German control. The enemy armoured car, described as a big, lumbering machine, was probably one of the solid-tyred, four-wheel-drive Ehrhardts or Daimlers favoured by the Germans. Nevertheless speeds exceeding fifty miles per hour were reached during the chase, which resulted in the capture of all the enemy vehicles.

The four armoured cars of 6 AMB were despatched in two instalments to Salonika in the early months of 1916, to join the Allied force which was supposed to be attacking Bulgaria from the south. The offensive never really got off the ground but, even if it had, the mountainous terrain would hardly have been an ideal place for the cars to work.

Some fifteen months later the battery was withdrawn and proceeded via Egypt to Mesopotamia.

British interest in Mesopotamia was founded primarily on the need to protect oil supplies, and operations there were controlled by the Indian Army. An early, dramatic advance up the Tigris, masterminded by General Sir Charles Townshend, carried a small force, supported by river gunboats, to the ancient site of Ctesiphon. A battle here, in November 1915, halted the British advance. Two armoured cars, probably Indian-type Fiats, formed part of a Flying Column under General Mellis but they failed to have any significant effect on events and Townshend was obliged to withdraw to Kut-al-Amara where he remained, beseiged, until he was forced to surrender in the following April.

In due course the fighting in this unhealthy, unprepossessing region absorbed an increasingly significant amount of British military effort and returned an equally daunting

93 *Part of the Hedjaz Section operating with Lawrence of Arabia. On the left a Ford T, then a Rolls-Royce armoured and a tender; on the right some gun carrying Talbot tenders of No. 10 Motor Section, RFA.*

94 *Rolls-Royce armoured cars and motorcycles of 12 LAMB on Egyptian State Railways wagons.*

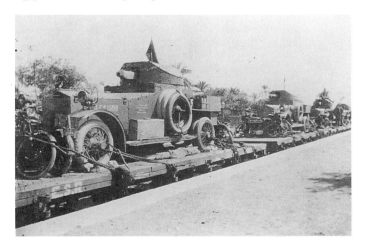

95 *An unidentified armoured vehicle, probably built locally, in service with a British unit in the Western Desert.*

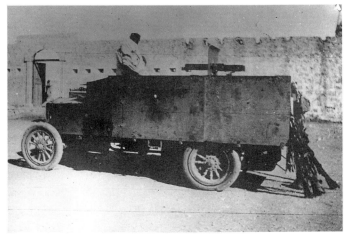

96 *The crew of this Rolls-Royce relax outside the American College at Aintab in Kurdistan. The picture was taken in July 1919 but it is typical of the units that operated in Mesopotamia.*

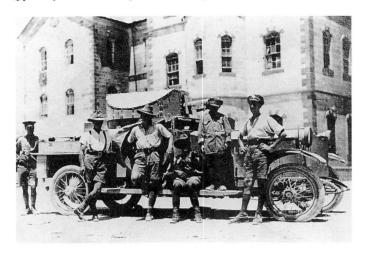

number of casualties, especially from disease. British armoured car batteries began to arrive in January 1917 and more kept appearing as they were withdrawn from other fronts. In all six LAMBs served in the region, all but one of them composed of eight armoured cars while the other, 6 LAMB, had six. The advance on Mosul was one long slog, with seasonal breaks, from the spring of 1917 until October 1918. The cars were in constant demand although little of their involvement could be described as spectacular.

The most important British armoured car of the First World War was undoubtedly the Rolls-Royce. In terms of numbers built, effective design and all-round quality it was unequalled, and is now taken to typify the vintage armoured car. However other manufacturers, seeking lucrative war work, also built armoured vehicles which were supplied to various Allied armies. Belgium was one important customer. With its own industrial centres in German hands the Belgian government bought most of its armoured cars from France but they also dealt with a British concern established exclusively for the purpose, the Army Lorry and Waggon Co. Ltd of Hayes, Middlesex. This firm undertook to purchase chassis from manufacturers and fit them with bodies to Belgian specifications. The majority were trucks with specialized fittings like ice-making equipment, but they also produced a few armoured cars. The chassis chosen was the six-cylinder Sheffield-Simplex and the armour was supplied by Cammell-Laird. The design of the cars owed little to current British practice, showing considerable French influence instead. The body was well shaped, low and sleek at the front with sloping radiator doors, well-ventilated engine covers and a series of large, hinged panels and doors for the crew. The turret looked like a massive wedge, open at the rear, which would have carried a Hotchkiss machine gun in service. The extent to which they were used by the Belgian army is not clear, the British firm was wound up early in 1916 and even the number of cars

completed is not known. The Belgians also seem to have operated some Lanchesters alongside their own open-topped Minervas and towards the end of the war fielded two British-made Lacre lorries fitted, it is believed, with locally built bodies.

The other country to purchase British armoured cars was Russia, indeed if one includes chassis purchased for completion as armoured cars in Russian factories, they had more than the British services did. Russian interest in armoured vehicles dates back well before the First World War and, considering the quality of their roads and the tremendous range of weather conditions, the use they made of them is nothing short of astounding. There is no doubt that this dashing style of warfare suited certain aspects of the Russian character but, unfortunately, it was not complemented by a devotion to maintenance work or even sound tactical doctrines. While a car would run it was used vigorously but once it broke down it was pushed aside and ignored. In action Russian armoured car crews would

97 *An armoured Sheffield-Simplex built for the Belgian Army by the Army Motor Lorry & Waggon Company of Hayes. The open-backed turret is facing rearwards.*

98 *The famous racing driver Charles Jarrott stands alongside an enormous Isotta-Fraschini which his company built for the Russians.*

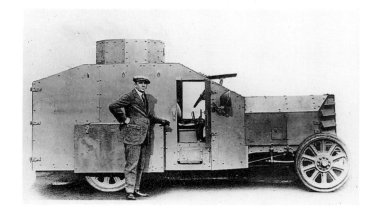

44

cheerfully charge directly at enemy trenches in a style more suited to a tank, and paid a heavy price accordingly. At its height the Russian armoured car force numbered over three hundred vehicles although the quantity available for action at any one time was probably only a fraction of this figure.

In 1914 the Imperial Government probably had no firm ideas about armoured car design and allowed contractors a free rein. Although they were obviously unimpressed by the pre-war model supplied by Armstrong-Whitworths they continued to patronize British suppliers and solicited a design from the famous racing driver Charles Jarrott. His firm, Jarrott and Letts, was a subsidiary of the Crossley Company in Manchester but they did not recommend that make of chassis. In any case Crossleys had landed a huge contract with the Royal Flying Corps, who probably claimed priority. Instead they chose the enormous 100 hp Issotta-Fraschini from Italy, a four-cylinder, chain-drive type which, in theory, had all the power in the world to spare. The hull was designed on the grand scale, which must have absorbed a good deal of this power, and it betrays a typical civilian concept of the armoured car as an all-purpose fighting vehicle, more along the lines of a tank. Armour covered everywhere except the front wheels, and the body was large enough to contain nine men, although the armament was limited to two machine guns, one in the turret and another in the rear of the hull. Thirty cars are said to have been ordered although how many were completed and despatched to Russia is not known. In any event they did not impress the Imperial army when they arrived and it would hardly be surprising to learn that a car of this size and weight, let loose on a typical Russian road, would sink like a stone into the first muddy puddle that it came to.

An altogether more sensible design was produced by the Sheffield-Simplex Company with armour fitted by Thomas Piggot and Co. of Birmingham. The chassis was the same type supplied to the Belgian army and the front end of the Russian cars was of a similar pattern. However the hull itself was a novel design which may have been stipulated by the Russians. If this was not the case, and the design originated in the United Kingdom, then it had considerable influence on future Russian practice. Instead of one central

*99 A Sheffield-Simplex armoured car built for the Russians. The staggered turrets, a typical Russian feature, are clearly shown.*

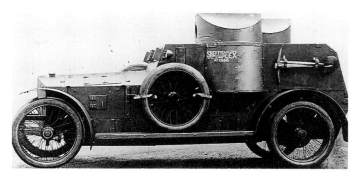

*100 On later versions of the Sheffield-Simplex, which appeared in 1916, a door was provided on the near side and the turrets set further back.*

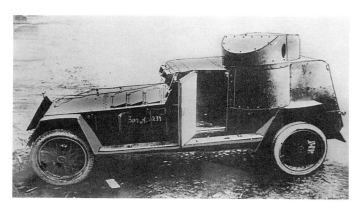

turret these cars mounted two small ones in echelon on opposite sides of the hull. Each was, in effect, like a miniature Rolls-Royce turret housing a Maxim machine gun with an arc of fire not far short of 360°. Although this implies problems of internal control and communications it offers the facility of bringing two guns to bear on selected targets, or the ability to engage two different targets at the same time. Two batches of cars, with slight variations in hull design, were supplied between 1915 and 1916 but, although the basic layout was repeated on many other cars in Russian service, the Sheffield-Simplex chassis proved less than robust enough for conditions on the Eastern Front.

A fleet of Lanchesters, practically identical to the Admiralty cars used by Locker-Lampson's force, was also apparently delivered to the Russians. They differed from their British counterparts mainly in the turret where a small cupola, in the shape of a cowl sloping downwards to the front, was fitted. This fixture was open at the back to enable a crew member to operate a small signalling device. Russian cars usually mounted the water-cooled Maxim machine gun and another local feature, often seen on Russian armoured cars, was a pair of sheet metal wings, projecting from either side of the gun aperture to protect the vulnerable water-jacket on the barrel from small arms fire. Some of these Lanchesters appear to have been fitted with a short 37 mm cannon in place of the machine gun, a practice which was quite common in French and Belgian units, from whom the Russians may have borrowed the idea.

The Russian government was soon importing chassis from manufacturers in many countries but one of the largest orders was placed with the British Austin Company. The make had been popular in Russia for many years and the first delivery from Birmingham included lorries, workshop vans, tank wagons, stores vans, ambulances and forty-eight armoured cars. The design of these cars, with their twin turrets and bulky hulls, may well have been dictated by the Russians although it was not as effective as the pattern seen on the Sheffield-Simplex and some other Russian-built cars.

101 German soldiers gather around a ditched Russian Lanchester. Notice the raised cupola and the signalling disc on this car, which was a local modification.

102 A composite picture from an Austin advertisement, showing the first style of armoured car which they produced for the Russian Army. The detail view in the centre shows the curious stowage locker, in the base of each turret, for the spare wheels.

103 An early model Austin in Russian service. It is fitted with KT studded tyres for driving on snow and bedecked with foliage to camouflage it and a cover to keep it warm.

104 The second type of Austin armoured car supplied to Russia had a slightly shorter body and a modified cab that gave each turret a wider field of fire.

Armouring of the bonnet, cab and body followed normal practice with the chassis completely enclosed. Amidships, on each side, was a cylindrical sponson, the upper section of which rotated and contained a machine gun. Thus the car had two turrets directly alongside one another, a scheme which restricted their potential field of fire, as did the high roof of the driver's cab. One curious feature was that each car carried two complete sets of tyres. For normal road work, if such a condition ever existed in Russia, Dunlop or Palmer Cord pneumatics were used, while a set of KT studded tyres was supplied for off-road use. Those tyres not in use could be stowed in special lockers at the base of each turret sponson. Austin employed the chassis of their 30 hp 'Colonial' car which, with the armour in place, had a top speed of 45 mph. By 1916 a new model was on the stocks with a slightly lower cab that did not interfere with the guns and a shortened body behind the turrets so that the rear end of the chassis formed a shallow tray. This was doubtless done to reduce weight and it is also noticeable that this car did not feature the sponson lockers or the optional KT tyres.

Austin production figures for 1916 reveal that 179 chassis were produced for armoured cars but a large proportion of these were not completed in Britain. Russian thoughts on armoured car design and employment tended towards the use of thicker armour and they also preferred the idea of staggering the two turrets in order to command a greater field of fire. Many Austin chassis, therefore, were delivered to the Putilov Works at St Petersburg where they were completed in accordance with Russian ideas. The only drawback was the quality of local workmanship which often manifested itself in badly-fitting plates that failed to keep out small-arms fire in action. The chassis supplied from Longbridge also featured duplicate steering at the rear, linked by a pulley system to the front axle. This enabled a crewman to steer a car out of action in reverse should the

*105   Austin armoured car chassis, complete with rear steering facilities, ready to leave for Russia where they would be fitted with armoured bodies made at the Putilov Works in St Petersburg.*

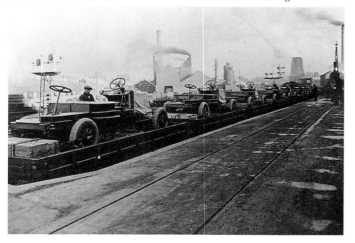

*106   A fleet of Austin armoured cars of the third pattern parade at the Longbridge works before departing for the front. These cars probably served with 17th Battalion, Tank Corps.*

need arise, which the Russian's bold tactics often demanded.

It is interesting to note that none of the Austins that were supplied before 1917, whether chassis or complete vehicles, featured double wheels on the rear axle. This was common practice elsewhere since it helped to spread the weight and reduce sinkage on soft ground. Certainly the heavier Putilov-Austin cars must have suffered from this problem since they were among the first converted by the Russian army into half-tracks. It is perhaps worth mentioning this interesting conversion since it affects some armoured cars that were of British origin. The manager of the Czar's motor pool was a Frenchman, Adolphe Kegresse, who devised and fitted a crude system of fabric tracks in place of the rear wheels on two of the Czar's cars, a Packard and Rolls-Royce. These proved to be ideal for operating in deep snow and a refined version was developed, in due course, for the armoured cars. Putilov-Austin-Kegresse types appear to have been the most popular, although other ideas were tried, and they were the nearest thing the Imperial army had to a real tank before the war ended.

By 1917 Austin had come up with their final design, the definitive version. Again the shape of the cab was altered but the main difference was at the back where the hull was stepped down behind the turrets, to provide the rear-facing driver with a better view, and continued to slope to the rear of the chassis. These were the first complete cars to leave Britain with the rear steering system and there is some evidence to suggest that later batches had twin wheels too. The upheavals in Russia, that culminated in the Soviet Revolution, brought all further business to a halt and found the Austin Company with some forty armoured cars on their hands, but these were suddenly in demand from another quarter.

Situated where he was, in the heart of Mother Russia, Locker-Lampson had ample opportunity to observe the Soviet convulsion at first hand. While still fighting a

*107   An Austin lorry prepares to pull a Lanchester armoured car back on to the road. A scene with Locker-Lampson's division in Russia.*

rearguard action against the common enemy he was trying to avoid direct involvement in Russian politics and extract his force safely from the country. This was achieved during the winter of 1917–18 but not without some excitement; all the armoured vehicles, which by now were in very poor condition, had to be left behind.

Meanwhile, in Mesopotamia, the effects of the Russian Revolution were also being felt. In one respect these were beneficial, since the Turks now massed their greatest strength in the north to exploit a Russian collapse in the Caucasus, but British forces on the Tigris also lost the potential support of a Russian force that had occupied north west Persia since 1915. This force had been slowly advancing towards the Tigris and had drawn off a large proportion of the enemy in that region. By early 1918 the situation was chaotic. All areas not directly under British or Turkish control degenerated into one seething mass of racial, political and religious factions, mixed up with pure banditry, that fell upon one another with a bloodcurdling will. A Turkish ambition to move into the area and corner the oil supplies led Britain to establish Dunsterforce, under Major-General L.C. Dunsterville, which would move through Persia and counter the threat. One element of this force, known as Duncars, consisted of the survivors of Locker-Lampson's division, now in Army uniform, under

the command of a Colonel Crawford, and the Austin armoured cars now languishing in Britain. A last-minute change of policy in the United Kingdom meant that only twenty-four of the forty cars actually reached the Middle East, so the remaining personnel formed motor machine gun units, transported in soft-skinned vehicles. Even then, the atrocious conditions in Persia prevented all but a few cars accompanying the force to its final destination, Baku, on the western shore of the Caspian Sea, and in the event it was never able to exert the necessary pressure in the face of enormous hardship. Ultimately the Turkish threat never materialized on the anticipated scale, so the whole adven-

*108   A pair of Austin armoured cars modified to run on rails at Ur Junction in Iraq.*

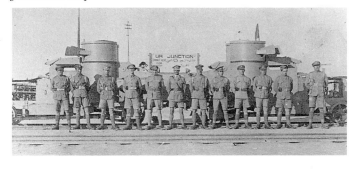

ture became a rather pointless exercise. The remaining
Austins in Mesopotamia later formed No.7 LAMB,
although at least two of them were incorporated into the
Railway Armoured Motor Battery, or RAMB, which
operated on the narrow-gauge line between Basra and
Baghdad. The cars were coupled back to back and fitted
with flanged railway wheels. They carried spare lengths of
rail to patch up the track in the event of sabotage and, for a
while, the names Valiant and Warspite, after famous British
battleships. Another car belonging to this strange, unsung
unit was Malaya, a converted Indian Pattern Fiat.

The reason that Duncars did not get its full quota of
Austins was due to a change of policy regarding armoured
cars at the War Office. Faced with the prospect of more
mobile operations on the Western Front, now that the tanks
had proved that they could break the German line, it was
decided to convert one battalion of the Tank Corps, the

17th, into an armoured car unit. Since these Austins, built
for the Russian government, originally mounted Maxim
heavy machine guns, and the Tank Corps favoured the
lighter, air-cooled Hotchkiss, the mountings on all sixteen
cars required modification while the battalion, which had
been training at Bovington Camp to operate Medium A,
Whippet tanks, was hastily advised of this change of plan.
The cars went from Cardiff Docks, where they were
awaiting shipment, to Bulford Camp on Salisbury Plain,
where the gun mountings were changed. Under the
command of Colonel E.J. Carter the best drivers were
selected and the unit made up to establishment and
despatched to France, all in under a month. Oddly, their
first location on the Continent was the region around
Poperinghe and St Omer where Commander Samson had
fought some of his early battles but a few weeks later, in
May 1918, they were withdrawn to the Tank Corps training
centre in France for a more thorough education in their new
role.

Throughout the early summer the cars operated with the
French and American armies. On numerous occasions they
were able to move forward, right among the enemy, to carry
out reconnaissance missions under fire in areas where no
other troops could survive. Thus they rapidly gained
experience, confidence and the admiration of the Allied
troops.

The great Battle of Amiens, which began on 8 August
1918, was the first move in what became the final collapse of
the German forces in the west. In the initial stages at least it
was a tank battle, on a scale that had never been attempted
before, but an important place was reserved for the
armoured cars. They came under the command of the 5th
Australian Division and their task was to cause as much
havoc as possible behind the German lines, paying particular attention to centres of command and, specifically, to the
Corps Headquarters known to be at Framerville, a town to
the south of the road that runs from Villers-Bretonneux to
St Quentin. The biggest problem was how the cars were to
get through the front-line areas – a maze of trenches and
shell holes that they could never hope to pass unaided. A
last-minute inspiration on the part of Carter led to a quick
experiment on the eve of the battle when, it was discovered,
a tank could tow two cars at a time, with very little
difficulty, since the wheels of the cars followed directly in
the tracks of the tank.

The part played by the armoured cars at Amiens was out
of all proportion to the size of their force. They were soon in
among enemy troops and transport, who could do nothing
but flee in all directions if they weren't wiped out on the
spot. Lieutenant E.J. Rollings M.C., commanding No.8
section, found the German HQ in Framerville, caused its
immediate evacuation and even nailed a small Australian
flag to the door as evidence of his visit. The events of this
day alone are too many to chronicle here. One car managed
to shoot up and stop a train while others even captured and
held two villages for a while, but their greatest value was in

*109   An Indian Pattern Fiat on rails which served in the Middle
East. It was named after the battleship HMS Malaya.*

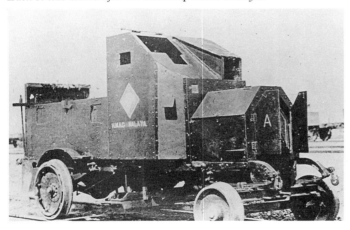

*110   Lieutenant-Colonel E.J. Carter commanding 17th (Armoured
Car) Battalion, Tank Corps with one of his Austins. At the time these
cars were painted sky blue and khaki in the hope that they would not
show up against the horizon.*

*111   During the Battle of Amiens the Austins of the 17th Battalion ranged far and wide behind the enemy lines despite German attempts to block the roads. This one is flying a red, brown and green Tank Corps flag.*

spreading fear and rumour far and wide. Unable to distinguish one armoured fighting vehicle from another, German troops reported a new British tank that could travel at 30 mph and spout fire in all directions; rumours like that are worth more than a cavalry division.

On 20 August the cars took part in the attack towards Bapaume in company with the Whippet tanks of 3rd Battalion, and this practice was employed on many subsequent occasions. The armoured cars worked well forward but, being restricted to the highways, could not pursue likely targets that made off across country; this was where the Medium tanks could assist. Casualties from enemy action and accidents reduced the effectives to six cars by the end of September but the majority were recovered and repaired, often right beside the road where they had been lost, thanks to the formation of a first aid detachment in suitably equipped Peerless lorries operated by the Battalion. The most serious problem was the chassis which developed weaknesses and often bent out of shape, but one of the criticisms levelled by the crews was the layout of the hinged driver's visor at the front. Unlike the last batch of cars

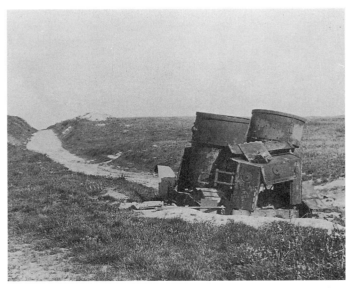

*112   The burnt and battered hull of Lieutenant Herd's Austin on the road near Aichet-le-Petit, August 1918.*

supplied to Russia, these latest Austins had but one vision-slit in the centre of the armour plate. Since this was closed down when operating under fire either the driver or the commander could peer through the slit, but not both at the same time. While the driver watched the road the commander had no idea of what was going on, and lost his power to command; if the commander wished to take a look the driver was forced to stop, otherwise it was almost inevitable that they would run off the road into a ditch.

By October it was clear that the Germans were retreating everywhere and the task assigned to the 17th Battalion was to turn an orderly retirement into a rout. One incident from this period deserves mention. Two cars working with the 6th Cavalry Brigade on a drive towards Le Cateau encountered a German demolition party about to blow up a railway bridge near Maurios. One car got across as the fuses were sizzling but the charges went off before the other arrived, leaving the first car stranded on the enemy side with no means of retreat. With everything closed down they proceeded to motor through enemy-held villages, shooting up anything they saw including emplaced mortar batteries that were expecting nothing less than a fast-moving attack from the rear. Approaching another bridge, which they assumed must be prepared for demolition, they made a surprise attack and chased away the German engineers before they could set the fuses. Returning via this bridge to the friendly side of the front, they picked up the other car and returned to company headquarters with a valuable report gleaned from a three-mile excursion through German-held territory.

The depleted 17th Battalion was in action right up to the time when the Armistice took effect but rarely with more than six or seven cars fit for service at any one time. The peace that followed gave the armoured car men little respite. Now they found another role for themselves which tanks could never do, and cavalry only with a vast expenditure of manpower. Mobility and economy of personnel were the key factors, for the regions beyond the final battle line were swarming with German soldiers streaming home and released Allied prisoners-of-war heading west. There being no organization to cope with this dual migration, a general shortage of food led to various incidents, and the armoured cars were a swift and effective means of sorting out trouble spots before they got out of hand. Arriving in the Belgian town of Charleroi, once the headquarters of the German tank force, they were asked to act as escort to a fleet of barges, bringing food to the town. The fear was that the cargo would be appropriated by other settlements on the way, so the cars took part in what they described as their only naval action, covering the movement of the barges from the towpath. A fitting finale, bearing in mind their origins.

The ultimate privilege for the armoured car men came on 6 December when eight cars escorted the Commanding Officer of 2nd Cavalry Brigade into Cologne to negotiate Allied control of the city. Crossing the Rhine by the Hohenzollern Bridge, with the leading car flying the brown, red and green Tank Corps flag, they made a fitting symbol of the victory of armour that had finally brought an end to one of the most horrendous wars in modern history.

113   *Following the Armistice the Austins, now marked with the white/red/white British identification symbol, escorted the British occupation forces into Cologne. Lady tram drivers were not only a British phenomenon.*

# CHAPTER 4
# Fighting Motorcycles

Searching for the origins of the armed motorcycle one might go back to Waite's pedal powered quadricycle or Simms' original Motor Scout, but the former was not motorized and the latter appeared at a time when the distinction between the motor car and cycle was blurred, to say the least. Another machine that should be noted was a small three-wheeler built by the Autocarrier Company of Thames Ditton. Four of these were hired by the 25th (Cyclists) Battalion of the County of London Regiment for exercises in 1910. Powered by a 5/6 hp single cylinder engine and with the driver perched above the single rear wheel, they had open-tray bodies at the front and were more properly used for local delivery work in urban areas. The Territorial regiment used them as machine gun carriers; two to carry ammunition and two with Maxim guns stowed on the cargo tray with extra crew members sitting precariously alongside them. However they could not be classed as motorcycles in the proper sense. In Canada, in 1908, Sergeant H.R. Northover, Quartermaster-Sergeant and Armourer of the 90th Canadian Militia, came up with something far more practical, a Harley-Davidson sidecar combination which mounted a Maxim gun fitted to fire forwards.

The first true armed motorcycle in Britain was a 3¾ hp Scott solo machine which was fitted, by the Coventry Ordnance Works in Glasgow, with one of their Laird-Menteyne machine guns. The object of the exercise was to interest the War Office in the new weapon and in the concept of motorcycle firepower at the same time, but it failed on both counts. Because the rider could not drive and

fire his gun, which was mounted on the handlebars, at the same time, a special tripod device was fitted so that once the rider had brought his machine up to the firing point, he set up the tripod to hold the machine steady, slipped from the saddle and began blasting away. Obviously the best answer was a sidecar outfit which was inherently stable and had sufficient room for the gun and gunner in addition to the driver, who could, in theory, fire on the move. The idea was bandied about before the war but, as usual, it failed to attract any attention from the War Office.

115  A Scott Maxim machine gun combination of the Royal Naval Air Service in the street outside the Wormwood Scrubs depot. A small White Ensign is flying from the handlebars.

114  Two of the AC Autocar motor tricycles borrowed as machine gun carriers by the 25th Cyclists Battalion, the London Regiment for their annual camp in 1910.

116  The limber version of the Scott carried a supply of ammunition and spare tyres for the fighting units.

When war broke out it was the Royal Navy, once again, who acted first. The Admiralty originally intended its motorcycle units to form part of the Royal Naval Division but, as the armoured car idea caught on, the five motorcycle machine gun squadrons (Nos 9 to 13) were included with them. Each squadron theoretically comprised twenty-four gun-carrying machines organised into six sections. Each section consisted of four gun combinations, four limber combinations with spare ammunition, four solo machines and one Ford car. The headquarters comprised a lorry and four solo machines while the first section had an extra staff car, section B2 a wireless car and C2 an ambulance. The motorcycles used by the Royal Naval Air Service were Scotts. They mounted Maxim machine guns of which each squadron had eighteen so that the fourth gun carrier in each section was an unarmed spare.

*117 Taking on aircraft with a Scott Maxim combination was not impossible, but it was decidedly uncomfortable.*

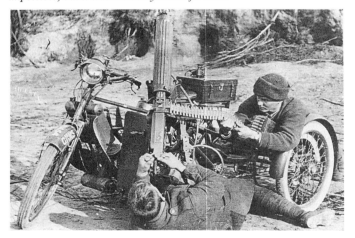

Scott motorcycles were manufactured in Bradford, and were very unconventional 532 cc water-cooled two-stroke twins with a two-speed gearbox and kick-start, something of a novelty at the time. The machines supplied to the Admiralty were of the standard 1914 model but the sidecars were not. They were a co-operative design by Alfred Scott himself and Sir Arthur Dawson of Vickers. Indeed, Vickers initiated the whole idea in order to produce a suitable mobile mount for their Maxim guns. The object of the design, which was jointly patented in August 1914, was to make the sidecar sturdy yet flexible enough to act as a tripod from which the Maxim could be fired without the need to dismount it. Protection for the crew was limited to a two-piece shield at the front of the sidecar while the rear, behind the gunner's seat, was taken up with ammunition stowage. It was even possible to use the gun in the anti-aircraft mode but, in order to do so, the upper half of the shield had to be removed while the gunner was obliged to lie on the ground and the driver acted as loader. The limber combinations needed only one crewman, the driver, while the sidecar, which had no armoured shield, was completely taken up by a tray full of ammunition boxes. Delivery was initially held up by the fact that Scott, like most manufacturers, relied heavily on German-made Bosch magnetos, which suddenly became a very scarce commodity. Production was only maintained by appealing to the patriotism of the nation's motorcyclists, who were asked to surrender their own magnetos on promise of a replacement of British or American manufacture, when these became available.

*118 This solo Scott machine towing a Maxim was another idea developed at Barlby Road which never caught on.*

Opportunities to use the squadrons in their intended role were few and far between. Apart from No.13, the reserve squadron which remained in Britain on home defence duties, the others all went out to the Mediterranean. This must have disappointed some of the early volunteers since the first two hundred were only accepted if they were physically fit, able to ride a motorcycle and speak French! All four squadrons spent some time at Gallipoli where they served as conventional machine gun troops because there was nowhere for them to use motorcycles. No.10 left first for Alexandria where it was duly absorbed into the Emergency Squadron while the other three were broken up and their personnel transferred to the flying branch. Only one experimental modification is known involving a solo Scott. This was fitted up at Wormwood Scrubs with a light, two-wheeled trailer mounting a Maxim gun but it does not seem to have been used operationally.

Although the War Office employed motorcycle dispatch riders from the outbreak of war they made no immediate moves towards establishing combat units. A photograph of a 6 hp Enfield combination, mounting a machine gun, which was made for the South African Defence Force, appeared in the issue of the magazine *Motor Cycle* of 22 October 1914. Commenting beneath the picture the editor, Geoffrey Smith said 'We marvel why large numbers of fleet

and mobile sidecars are not fitted up in this way' (for the British Army); by November things began to happen.

Following the Navy's example the War Office began by purchasing some Scotts, but the slow rate of production coupled with suspicions about robustness caused them to look elsewhere. A number of firms were already designing suitable combinations and producing prototypes, among

*119 Another forgotten name from the history of motorcycling was Premier, who supplied some machine gun combinations to the RNAS.*

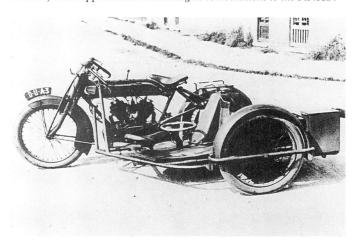

*120 No. 5 Battery, Motor Machine Gun Service, parade with their transport.*

121 *Despite the sleet, shoppers in Redditch gather to watch as a convoy of Royal Enfield motorcycle combinations leaves for the front.*

Indeed, Smith's office in Coventry was listed as the central recruiting office for men wishing to join the service and the *Motor Cycle* maintained a constant and fatherly interest in its brainchild for the duration of the war. Initially most of the batteries went out to France, where they formed a mobile reserve under Corps Command but, since the motorcycles were of little use once the trenches became established, the usual practice was to employ the machine gun teams in the trenches, particularly in vulnerable locations covering the join between two adjacent armies.

The Enfield Cycle Company of Redditch, Worcestershire, makers of the famous Royal Enfield motorcycle produced a combination mounting the Vickers machine gun. The sidecar was of very simple construction and designed in such a way that the gun faced to the rear, presumably to deliver the motorized equivalent of the Parthian shot. There was a forward position for the machine gun mounting but this appears to have been designed mainly for anti-aircraft shooting and, as with the Scott, the gunner was obliged to lie flat on his back to use it. By February 1915 a new version, based on the 6 hp Enfield, was available with optional fore and aft mountings for the gun, but it was never as popular as the Clyno.

The Vickers-Clyno combination was probably the best all-round unit of its kind to see service during the war. The motorcycle was a 6 hp V-twin, built by the Clyno Engineering Company of Wolverhampton. The sidecar was not unlike the version fitted to the Scott but it had one important advantage. The machine gun could be mounted on its normal field tripod and attached to the frame by

them Matchless, Premier and Zenith which do not seem to have got far beyond the prototype stage, and Enfield and Clyno which entered production. By December 1914 the War Office had formed the Motor Machine Gun Service to operate them. They were organised into six-gun batteries, each of eighteen motorcycle combinations (including spare and ammunition sidecars), a sidecar unit for the battery commander, eight solo machines (usually Triumphs) and two or three light wagons or vans. All told some two dozen batteries were raised over the next twelve months, largely with the help of Geoffrey Smith and his magazine which spread the word amongst competition and TT riders.

122 *Men and machines (Royal Enfields) pose near the station at Siberia Camp, Bisley during training.*

*123 A corporal of the Machine Gun Corps demonstrates the rearward mounted machine gun on a Royal Enfield at the works.*

*124 Vickers-Clyno combinations in France. In due course many of these men would transfer to the Tank Corps as the batteries disbanded.*

special quick-release clips, arranged so that it could be fired with equal facility in either direction. Also, of course, it meant that the entire gun and tripod assembly could be easily removed to fire dismounted (which soon became standard practice) and, just as important, it could be refitted very quickly if a hasty departure was called for. The officer commanding No.2 Section, 11th MMGS wrote, in his battle report; 'These machines were absolutely to be depended upon all through the operations. Their carrying capacities being great; at times the machines were overloaded with wounded infantry, especially the withdrawal from Fremicourt on the 24th when not only did they carry guns, full equipment and ammunition, but as many as four men. Some of the machines which were literally perforated with shrapnel still carried on, great credit being due to the ASC mechanics who repaired the bicycles in all places and under all conditions. Had it not been for these machines I am certain that the six guns would not be intact at the present

moment, owing to the reduced personnel of the teams.'

The original intention of the War Office had been to provide one battery of the Motor Machine Gun Service to each infantry division, one to each brigade of the Royal Field Artillery and the Royal Horse Artillery. In fact the MMGS was absorbed into the Machine Gun Corps when that organisation was formed late in 1915, but the majority of batteries were disbanded about a year later. Of those that survived, two went out to Italy, one to Palestine and five stayed in France. The battery in Palestine, No.17, soon discovered that its machines were virtually useless in the sand so it converted the Studebaker light trucks of its transport element into machine gun carriers and used them instead. The personnel from those batteries that disbanded in 1916 were transferred to a new formation, the Heavy Branch, Machine Gun Corps, known better by its later title, the Tank Corps.

The five surviving batteries on the Western front hardly ever hit the headlines since they became more or less trench-bound. Smith did his journalistic utmost to keep them in the public eye and to persuade his readers that they had not, as most people reasonably supposed, been abandoned altogether. His faithfulness was rewarded in 1918. The massive German assault on the Allied trenches, known as the March Offensive, called for as much mobility as could be quickly assembled so the men of the MMGS were hastily reunited with their Clynos. They were ideally suited to their new role, carrying out reconnaissance missions and acting as mobile rearguards for infantry units and artillery batteries about to be overwhelmed by advancing German storm-troopers. Although the guns, with their heavy tripods, were

*125 Firing on the move from a Vickers-Clyno would be a wild and inaccurate business, only practised in an emergency.*

126 & 127   *Two views of a Scott Guncar showing its interesting layout and the way that the gunner's chain-mail seat could be reversed.*

difficult enough to handle in the muddy conditions they usually operated dismounted with the combinations brought up as close as possible in readiness for the order to retire.

One incident from this period typifies the spirit of the Service and the durability of the Clyno. A press report of April 1918 tells how an unidentified battery held the outskirts of an anonymous village on the River Lys during a German attack. Early in the morning, a sergeant and two men went, with their Clyno combination, to investigate the other end of the village. They were soon joined by another machine under the command of an officer but, after firing for a while the latter was wounded by a sniper. An enemy machine gun now joined in the fight and the sergeant, seeing that desperate measures were called for, gathered up some infantry and, with some of them hanging on to the machine, proceeded along the street, firing on the move. They soon encountered the sniper who was about to give up the fight when the sergeant got him with a snap shot from his revolver. The enemy machine gun was taken and turned on the fleeing Germans while a wounded British prisoner

was rescued and about fifty Germans captured. Returning to the British end of the village a further twenty prisoners were taken.

As soon as the production of Scott motorcycle combinations was securely under way the firm's proprietor, Alfred Scott, left the company to look after itself while he set out to build a more suitable machine to his own design. A prototype was ready by the spring of 1915, followed by two pre-production machines which were christened Scott Guncars. Although they retained the offset tricycle layout of a conventional combination they owed nothing to normal motorcycle design, being more on the lines of a very light motor car with one front wheel missing. The basis was an integral tubular chassis with a very low centre of gravity; the engine, a 5 hp water-cooled twin, was mounted just behind the front wheel and coupled direct to a three-speed gearbox with shaft drive to the offside wheel only. The driver sat alongside the engine rather than over it, while the controls, which included a steering wheel, were of the car type. The gunner sat beside the driver and the Vickers gun could be operated in either direction, so the gunner's seat was

*128   French officers gather round to view the mysterious armoured combination said to be of British origin. In all probability it was never seen again.*

designed to be reversible. Both seats were made of interwoven leather rings that gave them an appearance not unlike chain mail and were slung, like deckchairs, from the frame. In order to reverse the gunner's seat one simply unhooked it from the upper frame at one end and stretched it in the opposite direction. The provision of large mudguards, the engine cover, front-mounted radiator and windscreen gave the machines a distinctly car-like appearance. Disc wheels were fitted all round and a limited amount of ammunition could be stowed at the rear, below the fuel tank. Novel as they were, the Guncars were offered at a time when the front in France was almost static and the War Office, already trying to work out how best to use the accumulating mass of motorcycle combinations, saw no reason to add to their numbers, even with what might have proved a more suitable product.

In October 1914 the Golby Sidecar Company of Coventry released a picture of their design for an armoured sidecar combination. The machine was covered, to a height of well over six feet on the front and sides, by vertical panels with numerous rifle slits in them. Rifles stuck out from two of these slits and, since one presupposes there was a driver as well the whole contraption must have been of a forbidding weight. Fortunately the armour on this prototype was only made of plywood, otherwise it seems unlikely that it would have got as far as it did along an English road, never mind into action in France. An armoured three-wheeler did exist but very little is known about it. The subject of one photograph and a contemporary cigarette card, it is shown, surrounded by British and French officers, as a low wedge-shaped machine with a machine gun at the front. Although it is thought to be British its parentage is unknown and its practical value highly suspect.

129  No. 20 Battery, MMGS converted one of their Ford Ts into a four-wheeled machine gun carrier.

## CHAPTER 5

# The Threat from Above

Typical British reluctance to modify traditional procedures in the face of technological progress is nowhere more apparent than in the field of military aviation. A few brave enthusiasts in both services did their best to prove the worth of the new arm but, even on the outbreak of war, aircraft were seen as little more than a local reconnaissance facility on land or sea. The idea that they might have considerable offensive potential was all but ignored. Only the Germans, through the efforts of Count von Zeppelin, took the possibility of strategic bombing seriously enough to do something about it and this was accompanied by an awareness of the need for a mobile form of anti-aircraft defence. Indeed, the earliest examples of motorized anti-aircraft guns to be examined by the German Army date from as early as 1906.

It has already been shown how, in 1914, the Zeppelin threat led, indirectly, to the formation of the first naval armoured car units in British service. Naturally it also stimulated interest in anti-aircraft gunnery in both the Navy and the Army before the year was out. To the Royal Navy, and in particular the Royal Naval Air Service, fell the task of defending the British Isles from airborne attack. Obviously the most effective response would be in the air, but adverse weather conditions and particularly the onset of darkness would ground conventional aircraft, while the airships could keep on flying. Certainly the Germans had every intention of raiding London by night so, as part of the commitment to defend the capital, Commodore Murray

*130    A selection of weapons outside the RNACD Armoury at Wormwood Scrubs. A 2-pdr Pom-Pom in the foreground with a 1-pdr Pom-Pom behind and a 3-pdr gun on the ground.*

Sueter raised a scratch anti-aircraft force with a motley collection of weapons manned largely by men drawn from the Special Constabulary and recruited into the RNVR. Some 6-pounder and 3-inch guns were used as fixed defence weapons while a few one-pounder Pom-Poms were mounted on lorries in order to pursue the raiders, or catch them in open country before they reached the city. Formed as the Royal Naval Anti-Aircraft Squadron, the mobile sections consisted of pairs of 2–3 ton Austin lorries, a non-subsidy type of very novel design. A typical section comprised a searchlight vehicle with a weak acetylene lamp mounted on a pedestal in the centre of the flat bed of the lorry and a similar vehicle mounting the Pom-Pom in the same fashion.

*131    A 1-pdr Pom-Pom mounted on an Austin lorry of the Royal Naval Anti-Aircraft Service.*

The first significant air raid on London took place on the night of 31 May 1915; it was relatively ineffectual in terms of damage done, but it alarmed the population and revealed the total inadequacy of the improvised defences which, on account of the public outcry, were immediately reorganized. The short summer nights seem to have discouraged the Germans from further raiding until early September when Zeppelins appeared over London on two successive nights, doing far more serious damage and killing or injuring well over one hundred people. Immediately the Government appointed the brilliant naval gunnery expert, Admiral Sir Percy Scott, to the overall command of AA Defence and he, in turn, found a very able subordinate. In

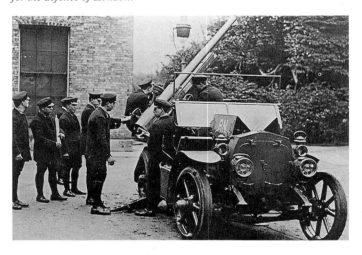

London at the time, recovering from a wound received at the front, was an officer named Rawlinson, a brother of General Sir Henry Rawlinson, an army commander in France. He was about to take command of an armoured car squadron, with the rank of Lieutenant Commander RNVR, but was quickly selected to take charge of an anti-aircraft unit. It was a happy choice since Rawlinson had been involved earlier in the organization of the air defences of Paris and knew his subject. This knowledge, combined with the urgency of the situation, enabled Rawlinson to take a dramatic step of his own devising. With the Admiral's blessing, but making no attempt to clear it with higher authority or the bureaucrats he left London by car on the morning of 16 September, arriving in Paris that night. On the 19th he was back in London with a French motor AA

gun and its attendant ammunition vehicle which he had personally persuaded the French Commander-in-Chief, General Joffre, to hand over to him.

The machines that Rawlinson produced with such dispatch were probably some of the best fighting vehicle designs of the war, for their purpose. Based on the 35 hp De Dion-Bouton chassis they consisted of a gun truck, with armoured radiator and bonnet, mounting a 75 mm (the celebrated *soixante-quinze*) gun, behind an armoured shield, on a turntable mount at the rear. The ammunition wagon, or auto-caisson, was the same basic design with a body formed of ammunition lockers and extra seats for the crew. The type originated in 1913 and the vehicle, powered by a V8 engine, was quite capable of moving at over 50 mph in pursuit of its quarry.

The gun went into action for the first time on the night of 13 October, following reports of a Zeppelin approaching the city. With headlights full on and siren wailing it raced along Oxford Street, driving buses, taxis and astonished pedestrians onto the pavement. Smashing its way through barricades where a section of the road was under repair it

135 *Lancia model IZ lorries mounting 3-pdr AA guns with their crews at Kenwood House.*

arrived at the firing ground in Moorgate in time to loose off two rounds at the airship, both of which unfortunately missed.

In due course this force grew to become the Anti-Aircraft Mobile Brigade, RNVR, but, on account of French demand for their own equipment, the supply of De Dion auto-cannons was limited to four, with just the one auto-caisson. A British equivalent was therefore devised. It consisted of a 30 cwt Lancia IZ chassis, a popular Italian type powered by a four cylinder engine rated at 35 hp. Totally unarmoured, it was equipped with a drop side body and a turntable mounted Vickers three-pounder gun. Eight of these were supplied although a ninth gun, on a special two-wheel trailer towed by another Lancia, was also used. Heavier firepower came in the form of a 3-inch gun on a high

136 *This Lancia towed a special mounting for the 3-pdr anti-aircraft gun.*

elevation mount fitted to the rear of a 3-ton Daimler lorry with special stabilizing outriggers. The Brigade establishment was completed by four Tilling-Stevens petrol-electric lorries mounting searchlights plus, of course, the necessary ammunition carriers and staff cars. Based originally at the RNAS depot in North Kensington it later transferred to Kenwood House, Hampstead, which was placed at its disposal by the owner, the Grand Duke Michael of Russia.

137 *The 3-in. 20 cwt, was mounted on to a Daimler lorry which was also fitted with a complex outrigger arrangement. Notice how the unfolded sides provide extra floor space for the crew.*

While on the subject of transport it is interesting to note the history and fate of one particular vehicle in Rawlinson's fleet. This was a tender, or light truck, on a Delaunay-Belleville chassis which, he tells us, had once been an armoured car. It seems almost impossible to doubt that this was once the turreted armoured car from 14 Squadron RNACD, the hull of which had been transferred to the Killen-Strait tractor by 20 Squadron to form the embryo tank in 1915. Rawlinson lost the car in 1917 during a visit to Foulness Island on the east coast; crossing the tidal causeway from the mainland he passed on the wrong side of a marker post and bogged the car down in the mud. Beating a hasty retreat on foot, he could only watch as the incoming tide and the glutinous mud slowly engulfed the car until it was out of sight. This move towards the coast was prompted partly by a desire to try and intercept the Zeppelins before they got to London, partly on account of the improved state of the fixed defences and, to some extent because of the supposed unreliability of the French anti-aircraft shells which, some said, did more harm to person and property than the German bombs.

The Royal Marine Artillery, like the Armoured Car Division of the RNAS, was one of those services within a service that seemed to thrive in a world of its own, despite the khaki anonymity of the Great War. A battalion accompanied the Royal Marines to Antwerp in 1914 but shortly afterwards it was withdrawn and split into two brigades. One manned heavy howitzers on the Flanders Coast while the other became an anti-aircraft brigade of four batteries. Each battery comprised four motorized anti-aircraft guns, two-pounder Pom-Poms on armoured Pierce-Arrow chassis. The lorry was a well built American type rated to carry five tons, mounting an armoured body by Wolseley Motors. A total of forty-eight were completed although there were never sufficient guns to equip all of them. The engine was fully protected with a large, hinged

138 *Rawlinson's team devised a special turntable for the Autocannon which almost turned it into a fixed mounting.*

139 *The Coventry Ordnance Works produced a modified, centre-trunnion mounting for the 75 mm gun on the Autocannon but only a few were produced.*

140 *A Pierce-Arrow Pom-Pom truck of the Anti-Aircraft Brigade, Royal Marine Artillery, with special wheel attachments to prevent it from sinking on soft ground.*

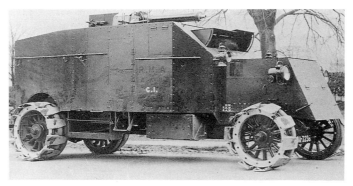

panel over the radiator, while the hull took the form of a large box, open at the top and sloped at the front, with the gun on a turntable mount in the centre. Two versions appeared, distinguished by the length of the armoured body, and some were fitted with wide flanges on the wheels which could be fitted with small metal plates to spread the load when driving over soft ground.

*141 Mounting a 1-pdr Pom-Pom in an armoured hull built by Vickers the Pierce-Arrows did quite well when they first arrived in France. This one appears to be camouflage painted.*

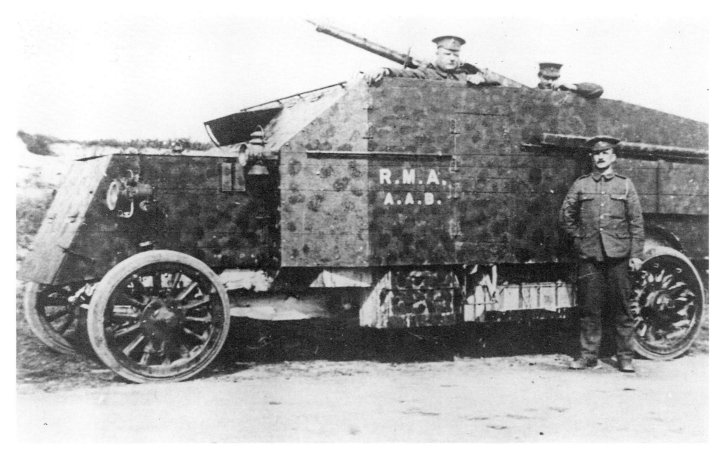

The success of the brigade was out of all proportion to its size although later in the war the Pom-Pom was outclassed as aircraft worked at higher operational ceilings. One battery, stationed near Dunkirk, remained in service until the end of the war although in 1917 it was re-equipped with unarmoured lorries mounting 3-inch guns. The other batteries served inland, alongside the Army, and these were taken over by the Royal Garrison Artillery in 1916. It is believed that some of the redundant armoured Pierce-Arrows were later converted into the three-pounder turreted lorries that joined Locker-Lampson's expedition.

Wolseley Motors produced a very similar armoured hull for the chain-drive Peerless chassis and about sixteen of these were sold to Russia. In addition to the Pom-Pom they carried extra machine guns for close-in defence and the top of the hull was partly covered at the rear. A picture of the lorries in Russian service shows that shields were fitted to the main gun mounting while at least one was modified by removing the Pom-Pom, enclosing the hull and fitting a small machine gun turret.

The British Army had no established anti-aircraft element when the war broke out but the need to counter hostile reconnaissance flights was soon obvious. By September 1914 some mobile Pom-Pom mounts were in service

*142 & 142a   Vickers-Wolseley built similar vehicles on the chain-drive Peerless chassis for the Russians. In this works photograph two auxiliary machine guns are mounted.*

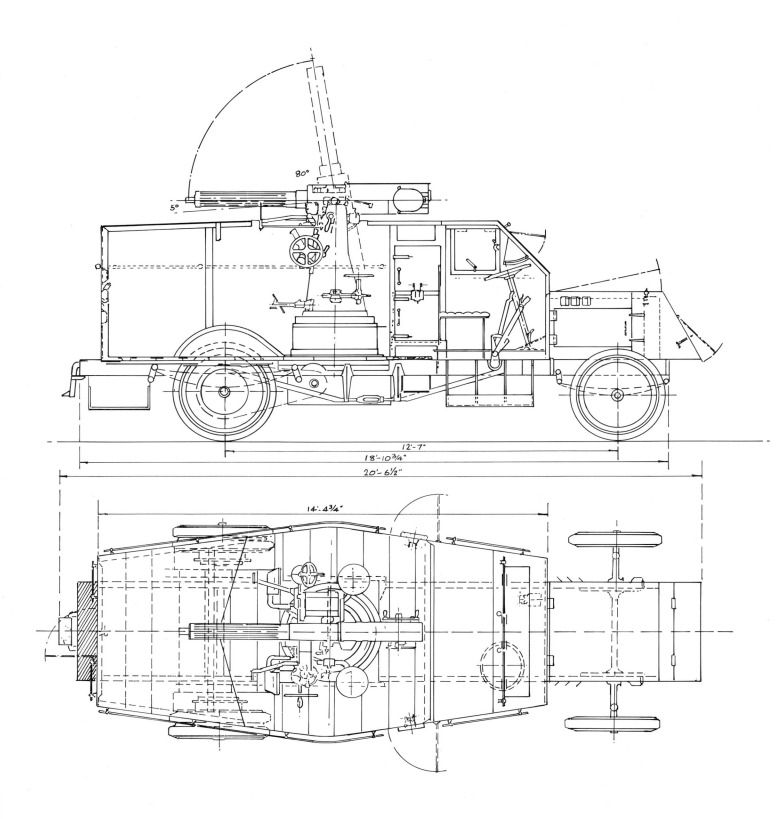

80°

5°

12'-7"

18'-10¾"

20'-6½"

14'-4¾"

*143 Two armoured Peerless AA lorries are proof tested on a rifle range. Notice that each vehicle has a different length of body.*

*144 This War Artist's view of British anti-aircraft lorries in action, early in the war, could show a type devised by Commander Samson or an improvised War Office version.*

with the Royal Field Artillery, but the need for something more substantial led to the development of the lorry mounted 13-pounder which first appeared in December. The 13-pounder was the standard weapon of the Royal Horse Artillery; with a calibre of 3 in. (75 mm) and a muzzle velocity of 1675 ft per second it had an effective ceiling, in the anti-aircraft role, of 17,000 ft. The conversion from field to AA gun was achieved first by fitting it to a high angle mounting and, secondly, by introducing a sprung catch to the breech which held the cartridge in place and prevented it from dropping out when the weapon was loaded while elevated.

The vehicles upon which these guns were mounted had no armour protection whatever. Most of them were standard British Subsidy types in the 3-ton class. The cab was the typical open style with a folding canvas canopy and an apron, extending upwards from the dashboard, which shielded the driver from the worst of the weather, there being no windscreen of any form. The wooden body was nothing more than a flat platform with low, hinged sides that folded down to increase the floor space in action so that

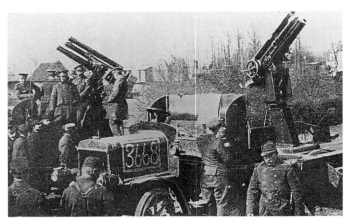

145   The first official mobile anti-aircraft gun authorized by the War Office was the 13-pounder Mark 3. Two are shown here on ex-LGOC bus chassis, being inspected by French soldiers.

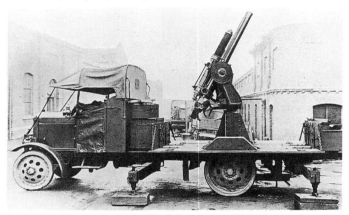

146   The 13-pounder 9 cwt Mark 3 was a modified 18-pounder seen here mounted on a Thornycroft J Type lorry.

147   The 3-in. 20 cwt was an excellent anti-aircraft gun which lasted well into the next war. It is seen here mounted on a Peerless chassis.

148   When the 13-pdr 9 cwt was fitted to the 3-inch gun mounting it was known as the Type 'A'. Here it is seen mounted on a stunningly camouflaged Peerless.

*149  The 13-pounder 9 cwt on the Mark 4 mounting was one of the most common types used during the war. This photograph shows two guns on Peerless trucks in action near Cambrai in March 1918.*

the crew could move around as the gun traversed, and a few small lockers for ready-use ammunition and tools. Retractable stabilizers of various patterns were a common feature; these would be unshipped and screwed down to rest on wooden blocks, placed on the ground, to steady the vehicle when it was firing. The range of chassis used included AEC, Daimler, Dennis and Peerless although the most popular types, probably because they were the most common in service anyway, were the famous Thornycroft J type and the S4X4 Leyland, known as the Royal Flying Corps model.

Improved weapons were introduced in 1915 but all, except one, were essentially conversions from various field guns of around 3 in. calibre with relatively short barrels which could only engage targets at around 20,000 ft. The exception was the 3 inch, 20 cwt Quick Firer which had been developed before the war. The longer (45 calibre) barrel had a muzzle velocity of 2,500 ft per second and a ceiling approaching 24,000 ft. The mounting, which included seats for the crew, was altogether more substantial and initially came mounted on a two-wheel trailer with folding outriggers. It was too heavy to be carried by the majority of British 3-tonners but in due course the American-built Peerless, which was designed to bear a 5-ton

payload, proved the ideal mobile mounting and remained in service until the late 'thirties. Many variations of the gun itself were made and they proved so effective that they saw active service throughout the Second World War as well.

The supply of guns to the front in France was always well in arrears of demand, even at the paltry establishment of two per division but, since aerial bombing did not become a serious threat until the summer of 1916, no great effort was made to speed it up. The original scheme was based upon a section of two guns with two more lorries to carry spare ammunition, a portable rangefinder and the crew. Two sections made up one battery. However this led to a demand for an inordinate number of battery commanders so, from June 1916 onwards, batteries were composed of four sections. A few AA Searchlight Sections, operated by the Royal Engineers, served with the guns but, since night bombing was hardly ever practised during the early part of the war, no great use was found for them. Things changed dramatically over the night of 20 June 1916, when a large scale air-raid was launched against a huge ammunition dump near St Omer, which virtually destroyed it. The importance of searchlights in forcing raiders to fly higher was rapidly appreciated and the number of guns increased

*150 Dazzle painted Thornycrofts mounting the 13-pdr 9 cwt Mark 4 halt by the roadside near Avesnes during the March 1918 retreat. A hasty departure no doubt accounts for the slapdash stowage.*

*151 This camouflaged Peerless mounting a 13-pdr 9 cwt seems to stick out like a sore thumb on a barren hillside in the Middle East.*

*152 A 3-ton Albion lorry photographed somewhere in Mesopotamia mounts a 2-pounder Pom-Pom.*

significantly. The regular practice was to provide each section with a close group of prepared and levelled sites, just behind the lines, from which to operate. However, once they had been in action against enemy machines they were obliged to move as the location was pinpointed and enemy artillery fire brought down. By then, of course, the anti-aircraft section had gone, but it was not forgotten, especially by the troops stationed in the area who had to bear the brunt of the retaliation.

AA units served on most fronts; there were, for instance, six sections with the Army in Mesopotamia and a total of fifteen accompanied the Egyptian Expeditionary Force on its advance through Jerusalem to Damascus. The normal procedure was for the motorized guns to follow in the wake of the advancing army, setting themselves up in stages to protect forward depots and troop concentrations.

In May 1917 the Army took over the responsibility for the anti-aircraft defence of Britain from the Royal Navy. They had been in charge of what were called the fixed defences for some time, but now it was decided that the various naval mobile forces should be taken under their command. London naturally remained the priority location and it was divided into three sub-commands, north, east and west. This last, the Western Sub-Command, was commanded by Rawlinson, now transferred to the Army. With Putney at its centre and including an arc that ran from Watford in the north, through Windsor and down to Bromley, it consisted of a chain of gun stations, observation posts and searchlights backed up by a small mobile element of De Dion auto-cannons and towed 3-inch guns.

Aeroplanes, particularly the relatively slow, low-flying biplanes of the First World War, were a tempting target to anyone who had a gun and often it hardly seemed to matter which side they were on. Thus, in addition to the regular equipment issued by the War Office it is not surprising to find that enterprising souls in many theatres of war took to producing improvised gun mountings of various types. In Mesopotamia, as already mentioned, the Leyland armoured lorries of Willoughby's battery were converted into un-armoured anti-aircraft trucks while at least one example is known of a two-pounder Vickers Pom-Pom mounted in the back of an ordinary Albion 3-ton lorry. Similar guns were mounted in railway wagons to protect troop trains and, of course, they were fitted to the flotilla of gunboats that supported the Army on the Tigris.

# CHAPTER 6

# Commonwealth Contributions

It is a curious paradox of the First World War that a nation whose army won, perhaps, the finest reputation in action was also a byword for indiscipline and one that hardly involved itself with mechanized warfare at all. It is true that, after a false start at Bullecourt in 1917, the Australians developed a close empathy with the Tank Corps in France but most of what they achieved was done on foot or, in the Middle East, on horseback. However they were not entirely disinterested in mechanization and even produced two armoured cars of their own.

A group of motoring enthusiasts in Victoria supplied three cars of which two, a Mercedes and a British Daimler, were fitted with armoured bodies by the Vulcan Engineering Works in South Melbourne. The third car, a Minerva, was completed as a tender while a motorcycle combination mounting a Colt machine gun made up the section. Both armoured cars were completely covered, with louvred radiator protection and hinged visors at front and back. One was fitted with a narrow, bevel-edged turret while the other had a large shield attached to the gun mounting instead. Colt machine guns were used in both cars; designed by John Browning, and dating back to 1895 they were known as 'potato diggers' on account of the curious action of the recocking arm, they were considered obsolete in 1914. The Australian Armoured Car Section arrived in Egypt in August 1916 but the cars, one of which was an old chain-drive model, proved unreliable, while spares for these one-off types were unobtainable. The crews soon transferred to Rolls-Royces and for some illogical reason the original cars were shipped all the way back to Australia. The only other motorized fighting unit of the Australian Army was a Light Car Patrol which operated in Palestine.

The proximity and influence of the motor-conscious United States probably accounts, to some extent, for the interest shown in armoured cars by the Canadians. This interest owed a lot more to individual enthusiasm than official backing but it brought results nevertheless. A typical example is a light armoured car built for the Canadian Volunteers of Victoria on an American Case car chassis. The Case Company, better known for their agricultural machinery, produced a range of four cylinder cars in 1914. This Canadian version looked more like a small pick-up truck with armour around the driver's cab and a Vickers machine gun on its tripod, fitted with a large

*154 One of the Australian cars, believed to be a chain-drive Mercedes, later had its turret removed to reduce the weight.*

*155 The other car, presumably the Daimler, carried a Colt machine gun behind a large shield but it was still rather too heavy for desert conditions.*

*153 The 1st Australian Armoured Car Section operated in Egypt alongisde 11 and 12 LAMBs. It comprised a Mercedes and a Daimler armoured car, a Minerva tender and a motorcycle combination mounting a Colt gun.*

156  Lieutenant Colonel Raymond Brutinel, founder of the 1st
Canadian Motor Machine Gun Brigade, served on the staff at the
British Army Machine Gun School in France. He is seen here pouring
over a map with Allied officers.

157  The Autocars of the Canadian MMG Brigade were strange
looking vehicles but they came into their own during the March 1918
fighting.

158  Used as static machine gun posts in an attempt to stem the flood of stormtroopers the cost to the Autocars and their crews was very high indeed.

shield, in the back. Although it was supplied to the Overseas Battalion of the Volunteers, there is no evidence to show whether it went to France or not. No such confusion surrounds the vehicles that accompanied the 1st Canadian Armoured Machine Gun Brigade to France in 1914. At the instigation of a retired French Army officer and early advocate of the machine gun, Raymond Brutinel, a group of wealthy Canadians funded what was, at the time, one of the most revolutionary fighting units put into the field by any country. Brutinel obviously appreciated that the machine gun could be an effective offensive weapon in addition to its more readily accepted defensive potential, but for this he needed mobility. He organized the Brigade around a fleet of vehicles built by the Autocar Company of Ardmore, Pennsylvania. The Autocar was a light, forward-control truck powered by a two-cylinder engine. Armour was supplied by the Bethlehem Steel Corporation and fitted around the cab while the rear part of the body was equipped with a series of folding panels and ammunition lockers with two machine guns, Colts originally, mounted on pedestals on the centre line. Twenty armoured vehicles were built and sent out to France, via Britain where Vickers machine guns were fitted in place of the Colts. They served with the Machine Gun Corps but, like most other mechanised units, found few opportunities to exploit their mobility until the German offensive of March 1918. Then, at last, they came into their own, dashing all over the front to bring their firepower to bear and seal up dangerous breakthroughs.

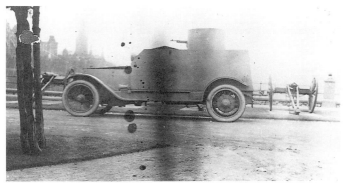

159 *Photographed in Ottawa the turreted Canadian Packard armoured car is shown in this poor, but unique print.*

Casualties were high because the Autocars were not designed to fight as armoured cars in the true sense but, rather, as mobile machine gun posts. Real turreted armoured cars, on Packard chassis, were designed for a second Canadian unit but there is no evidence to show that more than one was completed which, it is believed, never left Canada.

One of the most interesting commercial vehicles produced in the United States before the war was the Jeffery Quad, a four-wheel-drive, four-wheel-steering two-tonner built by the Thomas Jeffery Company in Wisconsin. Their

potential off-road performance interested the American Services and the Royal Navy, while a few chassis were used as the basis for some experimental armoured cars in the USA. When Sir John Eaton, a wealthy Canadian store proprietor, decided to raise a squadron of armoured cars for service in France, in 1915, the Quad was chosen and fitted with a bulky armoured hull with a driving cab at each end and a centrally mounted machine gun turret. Small sponsons, with pistol ports in them, were mounted on one side and the cars had a total weight of about seven tons, power being supplied by a four cylinder Buda engine rated at 40 hp. Forty armoured Quads were built and the deal was handled by the Canada Cycle and Motor Company of Toronto who traded under the Russell marque so that the cars were often known as Russells. They were supported by a fleet of soft-skinned vehicles, workshops and stores trucks, on the same chassis and a stylish, partly-armoured scout car based on a Russell-Knight tourer.

160 *The partly armoured Russell-Knight Scout Car from the Eaton Battery was a handsome looking vehicle. The fitting on the dashboard is a Colt machine gun mount.*

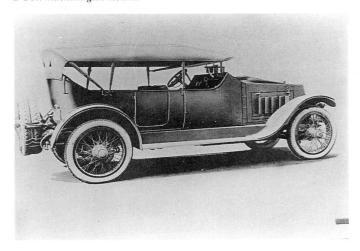

The Quads arrived in Britain in 1916 but, with the war in France virtually static, the Canadian Army decided that they were not needed at the front. For some time the machines languished at Bulford Camp until a scheme was put forward to convert them back into ordinary lorries. Since the Quad had fallen out of favour with the Royal Navy this plan came to nothing but by July 1917 the India Office was showing some interest. They suggested that the cars could be usefully employed, in their armoured form, in Mesopotamia and steps were taken to modify them for service in a hot climate.

The work was carried out by Hubbard Brothers of Basingstoke and a good stock of spares, retained by the Royal Navy at Shorncliffe, was released for them. The plan to use them on the Tigris front was soon dropped and shipments direct to India began instead but the SS Shirala, carrying four armoured cars, the Russell-Knight Scout Car

161 *Jeffery Quads of the Eaton Motor Machine Gun Battery are drawn up in the market square of an English town.*

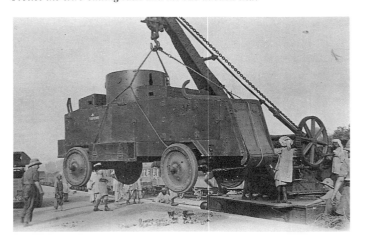

162 *One of the Jeffery Quads is unloaded from a train in India. Notice the wire-cutting rails and the cab at each end.*

and most of the spare parts, was torpedoed and sunk in the Mediterranean. Sixteen Quads actually arrived in India, the remaining twenty being diverted at the last minute to Ireland where a serious internal security problem had arisen.

The situation in India differed markedly from that pertaining in Australia or Canada. The latter countries, both far removed from the seat of war, enjoyed social stability which, apart from the wholesale departure of their young menfolk, remained largely undisturbed by events in the rest of the world. There had been conflict in India for longer than anyone could remember and such stability as there was owed much to the presence of the British Army. Commitments in Mesopotamia and France reduced this force to a mere skeleton and security soon became a serious problem. Disaffected elements within the country stirred up trouble while the warlike factions on the North West Frontier took full advantage of the situation. The answer to both problems was sought in the provision of armoured vehicles which could afford relatively few men protection, mobility and the firepower of many. In the spring of 1915 the Viceroy, at Simla, approved the formation of a number of Armoured Motor Units. In a letter to Lord Montagu of Beaulieu, the officer in charge of mechanical transport in the country, he suggested that they obtain some of the armoured cars 'that Winston Churchill so recklessly bought'! However, these cars were by then fully committed elsewhere so it fell to the Indian General Staff to supply their own.

Although mechanical transport had been tested for military service in India since the middle of the nineteenth century it had never been adopted on a large scale so the first problem was the acquisition of a suitable chassis. These came largely in the form of good-quality touring cars donated by members of the upper echelons of Indian society, who had a vested interest in maintaining the *status quo*, with the result, it is said, that of the forty or more cars

163 *Most of the armoured cars built in India from 1915 onwards conformed to a basic pattern but, as this picture shows the differences from car to car were such as to make nearly every one an individual. It also made them virtually impossible to identify.*

thus acquired, no two were of exactly the same make or model. The prospect of a quartermaster's nightmare was partially mitigated by the facts that the cars were scattered across the sub-continent and many of them were never actually used at all.

*164  A typical Indian Pattern armoured car is seen here crossing a pontoon bridge.*

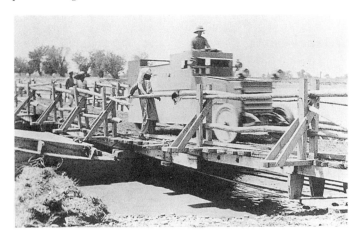

The plan adopted was to raise up to sixteen Armoured Motor Units, each three cars strong, manned by personnel drawn from local infantry regiments. Naturally the enthusiasm with which these arrangements were greeted depended, in the first place, upon the attitude of the general officer commanding any given area, while the constant movement of troops from one sector to another meant that the men assigned to the cars were forever changing so that many units were in a constant state of training. If a particular officer had no faith in the cars then the chances were that they would be shut up in some unfrequented corner of the local cantonment and left to rot.

Construction of the cars was undertaken in the workshops of various railway companies all over the country yet, despite this, a remarkable degree of standardization was achieved. Since real armour could not be obtained, boilerplate, somewhat less than a quarter of an inch thick, was used instead. The layout of a typical car consisted of a fully armoured bonnet with horizontal louvres or radiator doors, a cab with hinged vision ports and a short section of roof, while the rest of the body was open, with sides about 3 ft 6 in. high and a single, large door at the back. Wheel

*165  This photograph was taken to record the first visit by armoured cars to the Kohat Pass. The tall officer with his hands behind his back, near the centre car, is Major-General L.C. Dunsterville, later to command Dunsterforce. The date is May 1915.*

*166 Three armoured Rolls-Royces formed the 1st Armoured Motor Battery at Peshawar. Double rear wheels helped to spread the weight but the machine gun shields, which were later removed, made them top heavy.*

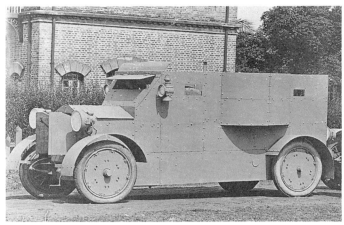

*167 The East India Railway Workshops at Lilooah, near Calcutta, built a batch of eight armoured cars of which this Cadillac was one.*

covers and wirecutting rails were common, if not universal fittings and twin rear wheels were used whenever possible. Originally the plan had been to fit one car in each unit with a machine gun while the others carried riflemen. Since the guns were also in short supply they could only be obtained by robbing the fixed fortifications which, it was argued, the cars would largely be replacing anyway. They were mostly ancient .45 Maxims and it was found that two batches of ammunition were available for them, dated 1897 and 1901 respectively; experience showed that the former was more reliable. Although the make, and often the model, of nearly every car is recorded, and a large number of photographs survive, it has never proved possible to identify more than a few of them with any certainty but, in any case, it would be impossible to describe all of them in a work of this size.

Selected vehicles will, therefore, be dealt with to illustrate the mixed character of the whole fleet. Probably the most famous, and certainly the most effective, were the three Rolls-Royces that formed Number 1 AMU, based at Peshawar. One of these cars was a company demonstration vehicle obtained from the agents in Bombay; the second was supplied by a wealthy merchant in Calcutta while the third was presented by the Rajah of Ticca. Armour was fitted in the workshops of the Great Indian Peninsular Railway in Bombay to the standard layout described above. The first two cars had flat sides while the third had rounded bulges about midway along each side. This was the machine gun car of the unit and the shape of the hull was chosen to give the gunners more room to traverse the weapon.

Peshawar, gateway to the Khyber Pass, was the key to one of the most troublesome areas in India. Mohmand tribesmen, under a mullah who declared a Holy War on the British with German and Turkish support, began to raid and pillage at once. Expert marksmen, as hardy as the barren mountain ranges in which they lived, who elevated warfare to the level of a national sport, caused endless trouble which kept the cars in action almost from the day they arrived on station. Their main duty was to patrol between the chain of stone forts and picquets that guarded the frontier, or to protect the flanks of punitive columns of infantry and cavalry from hit and run attacks when they moved out to quell an uprising. So important did this work

become that the unit was strengthened by the addition of three Minervas of very similar appearance, and an old Hotchkiss which could hardly move at all under the weight of its armoured body. Indeed, before long, the Hotchkiss was stripped back to a basic tender for carrying supplies ('mostly whisky' according to one veteran's recollection).

The Calcutta Presidency Battalion of the 1st Calcutta Volunteer Rifles obtained three Cadillacs armoured at the East Indian Railway workshops in nearby Lilooah. These formed the 15th Armoured Motor Unit. At first the cars conformed to the normal open-topped design with seats for six riflemen and internal stowage racks for their weapons. However, the opposition they had to deal with, in city streets with tall buildings, put the crews at risk, especially from the local speciality of dropping fizzy-pop bottles onto them from rooftops. So the cars were returned to Lilooah where they were fitted with high covered hulls that one observer likened to the shape of Noah's Ark. Firing ports were provided all around the hull and in the roof, with a

*168 In 1916 the Cadillac was rebuilt in what was called Noah's Ark form specifically for street fighting. It served with 15th AMB in Calcutta.*

*169 As this interior view of the Cadillac reveals it would be quite impossible to house all the men needed to handle the number of weapons shown in the previous picture.*

*170 8th AMB in Quetta operated this turreted Willys. It was armed with a 19th Century museum piece, a triple-barrelled, lever-operated Nordenfelt gun.*

*171 Another unlikely specimen was this Wolseley of 13th AMB in Bombay. The ludicrous turret, with its array of portholes, was probably an afterthought. The risk to the car's stability hardly bears thinking about.*

machine gun mounting on each of the four faces. A car was posed for photographs with all weapon ports in use, giving a total of four Maxims and sixteen rifles which, impressive as it looked, would require a crew of twenty-four in addition to the driver and commander! This was patently impossible and, even on well-paved city streets the cars proved to be dangerously unstable with a normal crew of five or six.

The desperate shortage of weapons was nowhere more evident than in Quetta where one of the cars, a chain-drive Willys-Overland, mounted a three barrelled Nordenfelt machine gun of incredible vintage. This gun, a lever-operated forerunner of the true automatic machine gun, required a long, triple-column, vertical magazine which fed the barrels by gravity each time the lever was worked and the gun fired. This necessitated a tall turret being fitted, with an opening in the top to allow the magazine to be changed. An armoured Daimler and a Minerva also made up the complement of 8th AMU in Quetta.

The Great Indian Peninsula Railway workshops in Parel supplied three armoured Wolseleys to 13th AMU in Bombay. One of these cars, of the conventional bow-sided

sort, also mounted an enormous turret-like structure which was drum shaped, open at the front and provided with eight or more large round holes about its circumference. It must have been fearfully top heavy and, if its stately progress failed to instil sufficient respect, virtually helpless. As far as possible cars of a particular make were stationed together for ease of maintenance, such as it was. Thus, for instance, there were three Daimlers with 5th AMU at Bannu, three Mercedes with 7th AMU at Lahore and three Austins with 12th AMU at Delhi. Others were not so fortunate; 4th AMU at Kohat managed with one Itala, one FN and a

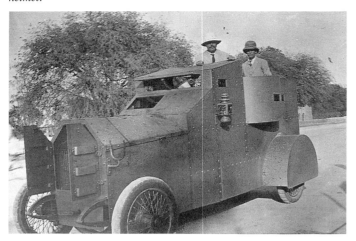

*171a   Colonel A.J. 'Tiny' Clifton, the officer in charge of the Indian armoured cars is believed to be the prominent figure in the white pith helmet.*

*172   Servicing was no problem, even if the facilities were a bit primitive. Set up the gallows, lift off the body and wheel away the chassis. A Rolls-Royce of 1st AMB.*

Minerva until these were replaced by three Daimlers in 1917.

The utility of the cars in certain regions was soon recognized and steps taken to improve their firepower by providing a machine gun for each vehicle. The Rolls-Royces at Peshawar soon had one gun per car, each fitted with a little shield. These cars also appear to have been camouflage-painted at some stage. Indeed they deserved all the attention that they could get because they proved so superior in terms of reliability that the Minervas with 1st AMU were sent elsewhere and a double-crew system adopted for the Rolls-Royces so that they could be used on a twenty-four hour basis if necessary.

By 1917 the units had been renamed Armoured Motor Batteries, although they still retained their old numbers. In the frontier regions particularly they were now organised into three-battery brigades except for 1st AMU which retained its individual status as a brigade headquarters and was reinforced by two more batteries formed from six Admiralty turreted Rolls-Royces that arrived from the Middle East. Tyres were an ever-present problem in India. They wore out quickly on the rough going, while stocks of

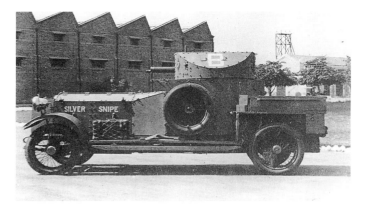

*173 Silver Snipe, shown here in the markings of the 7th Armoured Car Company after the war, was one of the British built Rolls-Royces to end up in India. Notice the loop-holes on the turret bevel.*

*174 Jeffery Quads in India were given a striking camouflage scheme. The bow shaped pistol ports were only provided on the left side of each car.*

spares deteriorated rapidly in the tropical conditions. It was by no means uncommon for a car to stagger back from a patrol with one or more shredded casings stuffed with dry grass in an emergency. Steps were taken to remedy this by fitting the new Rolls-Royces with disc wheels and MacKintosh NAP (Normal Air Pressure) semi-solid tyres although this was never done to any of the original Indian-built cars. Another feature peculiar to the turreted Rolls-Royce cars in India was the provision of a pair of protected loopholes in the turret bevels, through which revolvers or rifles could be fired at snipers in elevated positions in the passes.

The arrival of the Jeffery Quads from Britain eased the vehicle situation to some extent although, despite their four-wheel-drive, these cars were generally restricted to road work. They had never been designed for operations in such a hot climate and boiling radiators limited their range, making conditions inside almost unbearable. At about the same time the War Office in London began to take an interest in the supply of armoured cars for India. Sheets of Beardmore's proper armour plate were delivered. They were used to construct a number of vehicles that bore a superficial resemblance to the original armoured bus built at Woolwich, although they were somewhat shorter. The chassis chosen was that of the Fiat model 15 ter truck, an eminently reliable 30 cwt that was particularly popular in the Middle East. One of these armoured cars, as already stated, turned up in Mesopotamia at one stage, equipped with flanged wheels to run on the railway. In fact armoured lorries running on rails also appeared in India during the war. From Peshawar the road into the Khyber Pass runs through a wide valley to a fort at Jamrud, which marks the start of the Pass proper. Alongside the road ran a light railway which was patrolled by a pair of chain-drive Commer lorries, coupled back to back and fully armoured.

*175 Three of the Indian Pattern Fiats, assembled in India from plate supplied by Beardmores to a design worked out in Britain.*

Each lorry sported a small machine gun turret with a large roof hatch behind it to shelter riflemen. A sort of armoured corridor connection joined the two vehicles which, presumably, worked on the usual principle of the leading vehicle driving while the other was towed backwards until they reached the end of the line, where the arrangement was reversed.

One type of vehicle which was unique to the Indian Army was the armoured workshop lorry. A number of these were built on Fiat and Willys chassis to support the armoured cars and they were equipped with a range of power tools, electric lighting and extractor fans. The need for armoured workshops might be disputed in any other theatre but in India, where today's friend could be tomorrow's enemy, it was a different matter.

Although, by definition, Ireland could not be counted as a separate entity in the Commonwealth, the problems it posed for the British Government were of much the same order. The potential unrest posed by the Home Rule Bill had been laid aside in 1914 but, two years later, Republican aspirations culminated in the Easter Rising and the shortage of available manpower once again led to the swift adoption of armoured vehicles. There may already have been some armoured cars in the country. When they had first been taken over by the Army a few Rolls-Royce cars had been loaned to some Home Defence Cyclist Battalions which were stationed in various parts of the British Isles, including Ireland. However the emergency in 1916 called for an immediate response to a specific problem, the occupation of key buildings by groups of riflemen, and it resulted in the

*176   The push-and-pull armoured Commers that patrolled the Peshawar to Jamrud railway.*

*177   An armoured workshop lorry on an American Willys chassis. Each one came equipped with a full set of power tools.*

appearance of some of the weirdest armoured vehicles ever seen. The backbone of the fleet consisted of three Daimler lorries belonging to the Guinness Brewery in Dublin. They were taken to the workshops of the Great Southern Railway at Inchicore where the first one was completed for service on the very same day. Naturally the fitters at Inchicore could only work with the materials immediately to hand – the parts from steam locomotives – so the body of each vehicle was made simply from four smokeboxes held together by strips of steel bolted to the outside. A smokebox door, fitted to the open end of the rearmost unit, provided access to the fighting compartment and also contained a machine gun mounting which faced backwards. The driving compartment and bonnet had a covering of steel plates while a complete locomotive cab roof rested on top. Firing slits were cut into the sides of the body for observation and rifle fire but, in order to confuse snipers, many false slits were painted on as well. Two other lorries, armoured all over with flat steel plates, joined the fleet in due course but all five were used in more or less the same way. Although they proved useful for patrolling the streets their main function was more akin to that of the Trojan Horse. In order to deal with an occupied building the lorry was reversed up to the door, using its machine gun if necessary. The smokebox door was then opened so that the troops could storm the building with the minimum risk to themselves.

Although the Rising was put down fairly quickly it left a legacy of bitterness which continued until the formation of the Free State and beyond so that armoured vehicles became a permanent part of the Irish scene. The arrival of twenty Jeffery Quads has already been recounted but once the war ended other types started to appear. Indeed the ending of the war, in November 1918, did little to relieve the dangerous duties faced by the men who fought in armoured cars.

*178   A rear view of one of the ex-Guinness Brewery Daimlers built from locomotive parts and used in Dublin following the Easter Rising.*

*179   Another Dublin Daimler, built mainly from flat steel plates. Many of the loopholes along each side were simply painted on to confuse marksmen.*

180　*A partly armoured 3-ton Albion outside a protected court house.*

181　*In 1916 an old Dennis truck was converted into an armoured car for the Volunteers in Hong Kong.*

# CHAPTER 7
# Soldiering On

At the end of the war the 17th (Armoured Car) Battalion, Tank Corps, with their surviving Austins settled down to a period of occupation duties in Cologne. They spent a peaceful Christmas in pleasant surroundings with nothing worse than a slight shortage of food and a sullen population to worry about. Then, in January 1919, they were dispatched at short notice to Dublin where they were destined to remain until 1921. They were now equipped with a mixed force of cars and tanks which were gradually replaced by a new model Rolls-Royce armoured car, the 1920 pattern. By this time they had changed their title and become the 5th Armoured Car Company, Tank Corps, since the War Office finally decided that the operation of all armoured fighting vehicles should be placed under the control of one branch of the service.

The upheaval wrought within the British Army by the restoration of peace was almost as cataclysmic as the outbreak of war itself. Mixed in with the complications of mass demobilization were the problems of what to do with the new arms of service which had not existed before 1914. The Tank Corps was a prime example; there were those who contended that it only appeared in the first place to deal with a specific problem which, since it would never occur again, rendered the Corps and its tanks obsolete. Others were not even that subtle, regarding the war as an aberration that had interrupted the traditional business of soldiering which could only be restored by the total abolition of anything that had infected the Army since the summer of 1914. The Tank Corps managed to hang on, with difficulty, but the Machine Gun Corps did not; it was demobilised in 1920 and with it went administrative responsibility for a fleet of armoured cars that were still performing valuable security duties all over the world. The problem was solved by the formation of a series of armoured car companies manned by regular soldiers from those tank battalions that were not destined to survive into peacetime. It was a temporary solution; the Corps itself was only reprieved until 1923 on a reduced establishment of five

*182   In 1919 some new Rolls-Royce armoured cars appeared, identical to the 1914 pattern but with a larger turret. One is seen here in the centre of this group, sporting a smart camouflage scheme. The picture was taken in the Middle East around 1920.*

183 *During the Third Afghan War in 1919 Jeffery Quad armoured cars were used to smash holes – improvised field gun emplacements – in the walls of some frontier forts.*

184 *Armoured Car No. 2641 was one of the original Indian Rolls-Royces rebuilt at Jubbulpore in 1919. It now had a fully enclosed hull and an angular turret. In 1920 it was christened 'Wedding Bells'.*

185 *The camp at Parachinar in 1919, during the Third Afghan War. In addition to the Rolls-Royces and the motorcycle machine gun battery one should notice the old car in the foreground. It is a Hotchkiss, once an armoured car of 1st AMB now converted to a supply tender.*

*186 Austin armoured cars of 11th AMB return from Fort Sandeman in Baluchistan. These cars were all veterans of the fighting in the Middle East.*

battalions, and what would happen after that was anyone's guess. In the event, the future was assured by 1923 with the formation of the Royal Tank Corps which included a total of twelve armoured car companies.

Since this study is limited to those armoured cars built and operated during the First World War the full history of these companies has no place here. However, some wartime cars, particularly the Rolls-Royces, remained in service for many years and it is fitting that their ultimate fate should be set down. In Britain the end came quickly enough. A new breed of Rolls-Royce was coming into service during 1920 and the first of these went straight to Ireland. Here they were joined by a type of car which, although it was of post-war construction, owed everything to wartime influence. The Peerless was, indeed, no more than the chassis of the famous chain-drive American truck fitted with a twin-turret type of hull that was almost identical to the old Austin type. They were massive, slow and quite hopeless away from a good road surface but they were robust and some remained in service for twenty years. In Ireland they replaced the Jeffery Quads, which were ready for the scrap heap, while in Britain they escorted food convoys from the docks during the General Strike.

The Quads in India were obliged to hold on a bit longer but the shortage of spares forced the maintenance staff to resort to mechanical cannibalization to keep a few of them on the road. A new and original design of armoured car was being prepared for India but, in the meantime, the Quads shared the duties with an odd assortment of armoured cars that included the six turreted Rolls-Royces, the War Office pattern Fiats and one of the original box-bodied Rolls-Royces, the 1911 model originally presented by the Rajah of Ticca. In 1919 this car was rebuilt at the Indian Gun Carriage Factory at Jubbulpore. It now had an entirely new body with a turret on the lines of the Admiralty pattern but formed from flat plates. It was christened 'Wedding Bells' when it was used at an officer's wedding and remained in service, latterly as a training vehicle, until 1940. When fighting broke out in Waziristan in 1919, involving the Afghan regular army more cars were needed in a hurry and the nearest available were a few tired old Austins, the survivors of Duncars, which were hastily shipped in from Mesopotamia. Unlike their sisters in the 17th Battalion these Austins still retained their original Vickers gun armament but in due course they were adapted to run on steel disc wheels and NAP tyres, which seriously affected their stability. Pictures of overturned Austins abound in contemporary albums and one was damaged so badly that it was stripped of its turrets and turned into a sort of semi-armoured pick-up truck or tender.

**187** *The Austins were later fitted with disc wheels and NAP tyres. Unlike their counterparts in 17th Battalion these cars mounted Vickers machine guns.*

**188** *The high centre of gravity and the narrow tyres gave the Austins a reputation for instability. Big holes in the ground didn't help either.*

**189** *Probably as a result of one such accident this Austin was rebuilt as an armoured tender.*

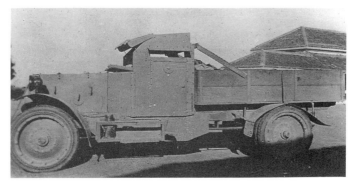

Meanwhile, in Mesopotamia and northern Persia the Bolshevik threat continued. The eight Rolls-Royces of 15 LAMB formed the armoured element of a new formation called Norperforce in 1919. It was despatched to Enzeli on the Caspian from where it was forced to retreat by a Soviet invasion in May 1920. The force remained in action for the rest of the year, slowly withdrawing in the face of increasing Bolshevik action while dealing with conditions that ranged from turret-deep snow to raging mountain torrents, often on roads hardly worthy of the name and, on occasion desperate for spares when the enemy cut the supply route to Baghdad. By 1921 15 LAMB was stationed in Basra as part of 1st Armoured Car Company, still with the same old cars.

Internal security duties kept more cars busy in Egypt, Palestine and Iraq, but the scale of trouble they had to deal with will be appreciated when it is explained that the first

*190   Rolls-Royce armoured cars of 15th LAMB took part in the Norperforce Operation between 1918 and 1921. A good set of spare tyres was a must in this rugged country.*

*191   The withdrawal of Norperforce became a struggle when melting snows turned the rivers into torrents. Grand Parade has to be towed out of this one.*

192   *Rolls-Royce armoured cars from 15th LAMB later formed part of 1st Armoured Car Company. The crew of this one encased the turret and crew compartment in asbestos to try and keep the heat down.*

193   *After the war many of the old cars in the Middle East had their hulls transferred to new chassis. HMAC Chatham of 1st ACC (although still bearing its LAMB badge) was one and it was later fitted with a wireless set and two aerials. The frame one on top of the turret works over a short range on the move but long distance communication can only be achieved by erecting the tall pole mast.*

two locations required only one Armoured Car Company each (3rd and 4th), while Iraq needed three (1st, 2nd and 6th) and kept them all busy. The majority of these cars were still 1914 pattern Rolls-Royces although new machines were arriving slowly. In the meantime, as a temporary measure, a number of new Silver Ghost chassis were sent out to the Middle East to be fitted with the armoured bodies from some of the older cars. Some of these hybrids lasted for a surprisingly long time. In 1922 the Royal Air Force undertook responsibility for the security of Iraq and shared duties with the Army in Palestine. Thus they inherited many of the surviving armoured cars while adding to their strength with newly built Rolls-Royces of their own. At the outbreak of the Second World War some of the hybrid armoured cars (1914 bodies on 1920 chassis) were still in service and one or two old bodies were even transferred to more modern Fordson chassis when the Rolls-Royces finally wore out. Cars of this type remained in RAF service until

1942 so it is by no means unreasonable to suggest that an armoured car body, built for the Royal Naval Air Service in 1914, operated by the Army from 1915 and the Royal Air Force from 1922, could have survived on three different chassis until it was scrapped, on Air Ministry instructions, in 1944.

*194   The Royal Air Force transferred their Rolls-Royce armoured car hulls on to Fordson chassis in 1940. The shallow sided turret on this one reveals that it began life as a Royal Naval Air Service car in 1914. Now it has an enhanced armament and a wireless compartment at the back.*

*Three Lanchesters and an Austin help to promote the Victory Loan Campaign in Birmingham towards the end of the war.*

# Appendix Summary of Units

This summary, compiled from War Diaries and other surviving records, is largely the result of painstaking research by Charles Messenger. It does not pretend to be definitive and in many cases it states the theoretical establishment rather than what happened in practice, but it does provide a straightforward reference to a complicated subject. Locations, equipment, dates and changes in unit title are all given where available, along with some educated speculation in less certain cases.

## Royal Naval Air Service

Eastchurch Squadron RNAS: improvised armoured cars and lorries. France, August 1914.

No.1 Squadron: formed October 1914. 15 Rolls-Royce.

No.2 Squadron: formed October 1914. 12 Wolseley, 2 Rolls-Royce.

No.3 Squadron: formed October 1914. 9 Wolseley, 6 Clement-Talbot.

No.4 Squadron: formed October 1914. 15 Clement-Talbot.

## Royal Naval Armoured Car Division

Formed at Wormwood Scrubs under Commander Boothby RN.

No.1 Squadron: 12 Rolls-Royce. April 1915 to SW Africa. August 1915 one section (4 cars) to East Africa (became 10 [RN] AMB), remainder to UK.

No.2 Squadron: 12 Rolls-Royce, 3 Seabrook. March 1915 France. UK late summer 1915. Early 1916 to Egypt as Nos 1, 2 and 3 AMB.

No.3 Squadron: 12 Rolls-Royce. March 1915 Dardanelles. June 1915 Egypt, less one section still in Dardanelles.

No.4 Squadron: 12 Rolls-Royce. April 1915 one section to Dardanelles. June 1915 remainder to Egypt.

No.5 Squadron: 12 Lanchester, 3 Seabrook. April 1915 to France.

No.6 Squadron: 12 Lanchester, 3 Seabrook. April 1915 Seabrooks only to France.

No.7 Squadron: 12 Rolls-Royce, 3 Seabrook. Retained in UK.

No.8 Squadron: 12 Rolls-Royce, 3 Seabrook. April 1915 to France.

No.9 Squadron: 18 motorcycle combinations. August 1915 to Dardanelles.

No.10 Squadron: 24 motorcycle combinations. Two sections (12 machines) to Dardanelles April 1915 as Motor Maxim Squadron.

No.11 Squadron: 18 motorcycle combinations. July 1915 to Dardanelles.

No.12 Squadron: 18 motorcycle combinations. July 1915 to Dardanelles.

No.13 Squadron: 18 motorcycle combinations. Retained in UK.

No.14 Squadron: 3 Delaunay-Belleville, 6 Rolls-Royce, 3 Clement-Talbot, 3 Seabrook. May 1915 Seabrooks only to France with three others as a heavy squadron.

No.15 Squadron: 12 Lanchester, 3 Seabrook. May 1915 to France, June 1915 to Belgium.

No.16 Squadron: 6 Seabrook. Formed in France in May 1915 from Seabrooks of No.2 and (probably) No.5 Squadrons. Operated with No.2 Squadron.

No.17 Squadron: 6 Seabrook. Formed in France in May 1915 from Seabrooks of No.15 and No.8 Squadrons. Operated with No.15 Squadron.

No.18 Squadron: 6 Seabrook. Formed in UK in May 1915 from Seabrooks of No.7 Squadron and three new vehicles.

No.19 Squadron: projected Seabrook squadron never completed.

No.20 Squadron: formed June 1915 for landship experiments. Transferred to Royal Marines in December 1917. Retained as tank testing and delivery organization until war's end.

No.21 Squadron: projected RN landship squadron never completed.

No.22 Squadron: projected RN landship squadron never completed.

No.23 Squadron: projected RN landship squadron never completed.

Emergency Squadron: formed in Alexandria September 1915 from sections of 3 and 4 Squadrons (12 Rolls-Royce) not landed at Dardanelles. Western Frontier Force November 1915 to April 1916. Cars going to 11 and 12 LACB from July 1916.

Russian Armoured Car Division: formed in UK October 1915 from 15 and 17 Squadrons. Organized as three new squadrons (Nos 1, 2 and 3). 1 Rolls-Royce, 33 Lanchester, 3 to 5 Pierce-Arrow and later 9 Fords and one more Rolls-Royce. December 1915 to Russia, in Caucasus 1916 and Galicia 1917. Under Royal Marines control from November 1917. Personnel left Russia early 1918 – became Duncars under Army control in January 1918.

RN Anti-Aircraft Squadron: mobile sections comprising one Pom-Pom and one searchlight lorry.

RN Anti-Aircraft Mobile Brigade: formed October 1915. 8 Lancia 3-pdr AA lorries, 1 Lancia towing 3-pdr AA, 4 De Dion Autocannon, 1 Daimler 3-in. AA and searchlight lorries. Transferred to Army in May 1917.

Royal Marine Artillery AA Brigade: 16 Pierce-Arrow in four batteries of four guns. Equipped between May and September 1915 for service in France.


## War Office

*Motor Machine Gun Service*

Formed at Bisley in November 1914. Used Scott, Clyno and Royal Enfield motorcycle machine gun combinations, 18 per battery with six Vickers guns. Originally in two-gun sections.

No.1 Battery: Scotts, France December 1914–March 1919. Absorbed into Motor Machine Gun Battalion.

No.2 Battery: France January 1915, disbanded October 1916.

No.3 Battery: France early 1915, Italy from October 1917, probably disbanded there late 1918.

No.4 Battery: France early 1915–March 1919. Absorbed into Motor Machine Gun Battalion.

No.5 Battery: Enfields. France March 1915, disbanded October 1916.

No.6 Battery: France April 1915–March 1919. Absorbed into Motor Machine Gun Battalion.

No.7 Battery: France April 1915–March 1919. Absorbed into Motor Machine Gun Battalion.

No.8 Battery: France July 1915. Disbanded October 1916.

No.9 Battery: France May 1915. Disbanded October 1916.

No.10 (Scotch) Battery: Enfields, France August 1915, disbanded October 1916.

No.11 Battery: France August 1915. Italy October–December 1917. France December 1917–March 1919. Absorbed into Motor Machine Gun Battalion.

No.12 Battery: France July 1915. Italy October–December 1917. France December 1917–June 1918 then, probably, disbanded.

No.13 Battery: France July 1915. Disbanded November 1916.

No.14 Battery: France August 1915–September 1917 then, probably, disbanded.

No.15 Battery: France August 1915–September 1917 then, probably, disbanded.

No.16 Battery: France August 1915–October 1917 then disbanded.

No.17 Battery: Egypt January 1917 with Western Frontier Force. Used five Studebaker cars with machine guns in Palestine, April 1917. Became 15 LAMB in June 1917.

No.18 Battery: France February 1916. Mediterranean (IX Corps) March 1916. France December 1916–September 1917 then, probably, disbanded.

No.20 Battery: UK some time in 1916. Converted to 13 LAMB.

No.21 Battery: Mediterranean (IX Corps) March 1916.

No.22 Battery: India from 1916.

No.23 Battery: possibly also in India.

No.24 Battery: France February 1916. Disbanded November 1916.

No.25 Battery: mobilized in India May 1917. Egypt July 1917–January 1918, then disbanded.

Motor Machine Gun Brigade: formed in France, June 1918, from Nos 1, 4, 6, 7 and 11 Batteries.

Motor Machine Gun Battalion, Machine Gun Corps: formed from batteries comprising the MMG Brigade in UK in 1919. Disbanded with the rest of the Machine Gun Corps in 1922.

*Machine Gun Corps (Motors)*

On the formation of the Machine Gun Corps in October 1915 the Motor Machine Gun Service was absorbed into it as the MGC (Motors), which included the ex-naval armoured cars. These latter were initially organized into four-car (Rolls-Royce) Armoured Motor Batteries (AMB). Light Armoured Car Batteries (LACB) or Light Armoured Batteries (LAB). Later eight-car Light Armoured Motor Batteries (LAMB) were formed.

Nos 1, 2 and 3 AMB: Egypt January 1916. Western Frontier Force March 1916. Redesignated Light Armoured Car Brigade (LACB) early 1917 with HQ at Sollum. HQ to Palestine November 1917–April 1918. Returned to Egypt, then Persia early 1919. Disbanded July 1919. Movements of individual batteries as follows;

No.1 Battery: Egypt until May 1918 less one section sent to Hedjaz Armoured Car Section which became a battery again when remaining sections joined it June 1918. Reformed in October 1918 after Hedjaz AMB disbanded. Palestine November 1918, Persia early 1919. Absorbed into No.4 Armoured Car Company, Tank Corps (4 ACC,TC) in June 1920.

No.2 Battery: with Western Frontier (later Desert) Force until November 1917 and sent to Palestine. Egypt May 1918. Western Desert Force in June and July 1918. Palestine September 1918. Egypt early 1920. Absorbed by 4 ACC,TC in June 1920.

No.3 Battery: with Western Frontier (later Desert) Force until November 1917 and sent to Palestine. Egypt May 1918. Benghazi Mission July–August 1918. Detachment to Sudan in January 1919, handed over to Egyptian Army. Remainder probably absorbed by 4 ACC,TC in June 1920.

4 LAB: formed in UK. East Africa February 1916. Egypt April 1917. Probably disbanded shortly afterwards.

5 LAB: formed in UK. East Africa February 1916. Egypt June 1917. Disbanded August 1917.

6 AMB: Salonika (with just two Rolls-Royces) in January 1916. Egypt May 1917 with two more Rolls-Royces and the four Leylands of No.1 (Willoughby's) AMB. Became 6 LAMB, Mesopotamia August 1917, discarded Leylands September 1917. Dunsterforce (Duncars) with six Rolls-Royces February–October 1918. Iraq November 1918–December 1920. Absorbed by 1 ACC,TC.

7 LAB (later LAMB): France March 1916. Mesopotamia February 1918. Takes over Duncars Austins November–December 1918. Still in Mesopotamia in June 1919, then probably disbanded.

8 LAB (later LAMB): France March 1916 with four Rolls-Royces and two towed 3-pdr guns. October 1917 absorbs 9 LAB. Mesopotamia December 1917. Kurdistan May 1919. Iraq October 1919. Absorbed by 2 ACC,TC in October 1920.

9 LAB: France March 1916 equipped as 8 LAB and absorbed by it in October 1917.

10 (RN) AMB: original detachment of No.1 Squadron RNACD. East Africa throughout 1916. Egypt January 1917 then disbanded.

11 LACB: mobilized at Bisley in May 1916. Egypt April 1916. Takes over four Rolls-Royces from Emergency Squadron RNACD. Western Frontier Force May 1916. Palestine March 1917. Under command of LAC Brigade December 1917–April 1918. Persia early 1919 then back to Palestine later in the year. Absorbed by 7 ACC,TC July 1920.

12 LACB: as for 11 LACB but absorbed by 8 ACC,TC in 1920.

13 LAMB: formed from 20 MMG Battery at Bisley in 1916 with eight Rolls-Royces. Mesopotamia December 1916. Persia January 1919. Disbanded when cars went to India.

14 LAMB: from UK to Mesopotamia in January 1917, Kurdistan May 1919. Absorbed by 2 ACC,TC in December 1920.

15 LAMB: formed in Egypt July 1917 from 17 MMG Battery and personnel from No.1 (Willoughby's) AMB. Mesopotamia August 1917. North Persia (Norperforce) October 1918. Absorbed by 1 ACC,TC in January 1921.

## Miscellaneous Armoured Car Units

1 (Willoughby's) AMB, officially 322 Company, ASC. Privately raised in February 1915, four Leylands. East Africa 1917. Disbanded July 1917.

16 and 17 Railway Defence Armoured Batteries: Mesopotamia 1918. Probably equipped with converted Fiat and Austin cars.

No.1 Railway Armoured Motor Battery (RAMB): Mesopotamia 1921, probably using cars from 16 and 17 RDAB.

Dunsterforce Armoured Car Brigade (Duncars): formed in January 1918 from personnel of the Russian Armoured Car Division. Mesopotamia March 1918. A Squadron (eight Austins in two four-car batteries) May 1918. B and C Squadrons (each with four sections of four Model T Ford vans mounting machine guns) July 1918. D and E Squadrons (eight Austins each) were not officially part of Duncars, went to North Persia in September 1918. Disbanded in UK March 1919. Cars went to India.

Hedjaz Armoured Car Section (later Battery): formed in May 1917 to operate with T.E. Lawrence. Initially two Rolls-Royces (probably ex-10 [RN] AMB), joined by two cars of No.1 Battery LAC Brigade in December 1917. Designated battery when remainder of No.1 Battery arrived in June 1918. Disbanded at Suez October 1918.

10 Motor Section RFA: formed under the LAC brigade in Egypt, August 1917. Six Talbot tenders and two 10-pdr guns. Arabia with Lawrence from November 1917. Disbanded November 1918.

17th Battalion Tank Corps: raised as Whippet tank battalion at Bovington in January 1918. Converted to Austin armoured cars (two companies of four two-car sections) in April 1918 and sent to France. Germany December 1918. Ireland January 1919. Became 5 ACC,TC.

1–6 sections Heavy Cars: France January–April 1916. Probably ex-RNACD Seabrooks in two- or three-car sections.

Motor Machine Gun Section, 6th Indian Division: two armoured cars and two lorries fought with the 'Flying Column' at the Battle of Ctesiphon, November 1915. Yeomanry/Infantry: some Yeomanry regiments had armoured cars built from private funds in 1914/15. Evidence shows that some infantry cyclist battalions had armoured cars (1/8 Cyclist Battalion, Essex Regiment had two Rolls-Royces from late 1915–February 1916). Seven Rolls-Royces went to Ireland in May 1916, probably manned by infantry and twenty Jeffery Quads definitely crewed by infantrymen went there in August 1917.

## Light Car Patrols (LCP)

Formed in Egypt in March 1916 as Light Car Scout Corps. Each LCP comprised five Ford T cars and a stores tender.

1 LCP: Western Desert Force May 1916, Palestine October 1917, Egypt June 1919. Probably absorbed by 3 ACC,TC.

2 LCP: Western Desert Force May 1916, Palestine October 1918, Egypt June 1919. Probably absorbed by 3 ACC,TC.

3 LCP: Western Desert Force May 1916, Palestine October 1918. 4 ACC,TC from June 1920.

4 LCP: Western Desert Force May 1916, Palestine September 1918. 4 ACC,TC from June 1920.

5 LCP: Western Desert Force May 1916, Benghazi Mission July–August 1918. Palestine April 1919, Egypt June 1919. Probably absorbed by 3 ACC,TC.

6 LCP: Western Desert Force May 1916, remained in Egypt. Absorbed by 3 ACC,TC in March 1921.

7 (Australian) LCP: formed in spring of 1917, probably from personnel of Australian Armoured Car Section. Palestine June 1917. Absorbed by 4 ACC,TC in June 1920.

8 LCP: Egypt July 1918. Probably absorbed by 3 ACC,TC.

9 LCP: Egypt July 1918. Palestine October 1918. Persia June 1919. Absorbed by 4 ACC,TC in June 1920.

Emergency LCPs: two such patrols operational in the Cairo district in mid-1919.

## Commonwealth Units

*Australia*

1st Australian Armoured Car Section: 1 Daimler, 1 Mercedes, a Minerva tender and motorcycle machine gun combination. Egypt April 1916. Attached 11 and 12 LACBs of Western Frontier Force in June 1916. Cars returned to Australia in April 1917.

*Canada*

Automobile Machine Gun Brigade (later 1st Canadian Motor Machine Gun Brigade) Canadian Expeditionary Force: twenty Autocars, raised September 1914. UK October 1914. France from February 1915, Canada 1919 to become 1st Armoured Car Regiment in 1935.

Eaton Motor Machine Gun Battery: forty Jeffery Quads, raised 1915. To UK 1916. Disbanded and cars handed over to Indian government. Some later sent to Ireland instead.

*India*

1 AMB: three Rolls-Royce, Peshawar 1915–1919.

2 AMB: one Hotchkiss later three Rolls-Royce, Peshawar. 7 ACC,TC from February 1921.

3 AMB: three Minerva, later three Rolls-Royce and a Lorraine-Deitrich, Peshawar. 7 ACC,TC from February 1921.

4 AMB: one Itala, one FN, one Minerva, later three Daimler and then three Quad, Kohat, 7 ACC,TC from February 1921.

5 AMB: three Daimler and then three Quad, Bannu. 10 ACC,TC from February 1921.

6 AMB: three Minerva, Bannu, Waziristan 1919. Joined 7 AMB in December 1919.

7 AMB: three Mercedes, later three Quad, Dera Ismail Khan, Waziristan 1919. Joined 6 AMB in December 1919. 10 ACC,TC from October 1921.

8 AMB: one Daimler, one Minerva, one Willys, later three Quad. Quetta.

9 AMB: three Sunbeam: Lahore. 8 ACC,TC from February 1921.

10 AMB: one Standard, two Napier later three Quad. Ferozepore. 8 ACC,TC from February 1921.

11 AMB: three Straker-Squire, Ambala. 7 ACC,TC from February 1921.

12 AMB: three Austin later three Fiat, Delhi. 8 ACC,TC from February 1921.

13 AMB: three Wolseley 16/20 hp, later three Wolseley 12/16 hp, Bombay. 10 ACC,TC from October 1921.

14 AMB: three Bianchi, one Minerva, Lucknow.

15 AMB: three Cadillac, Calcutta. 10 ACC,TC from October 1921.

16 AMB: three Wolseley 24/30 hp, Secunderabad. 10 ACC,TC from October 1921.

# Index

Printed in the United Kingdom for Her Majesty's Stationery Office

Dd 238639 C40 8/87